# HOW TO SURVIVE IN GEORGIAN BRITAIN

# HOW TO SURVIVE IN GEORGIAN BRITAIN

KIM SEABROOK

PEN & SWORD HISTORY

AN IMPRINT OF PEN & SWORD BOOKS LTD.
YORKSHIRE – PHILADELPHIA

First published in Great Britain in 2025 by
PEN AND SWORD HISTORY
An imprint of
Pen & Sword Books Ltd
Yorkshire – Philadelphia



ISBN 978 1 03610 853 3



A CIP catalogue record for this book is available from the British Library.



Typeset in Times New Roman 11/14 by
SJmagic DESIGN SERVICES, India.
Printed and bound in the UK by CPI Group (UK) Ltd.

The Publisher's authorised representative in the EU for product safety is Authorised Rep Compliance Ltd., Ground Floor, 71 Lower Baggot Street, Dublin D02 P593, Ireland.
www.arccompliance.com

*For a complete list of Pen & Sword titles please contact*
PEN & SWORD BOOKS LIMITED
George House, Units 12 & 13, Beevor Street, Off Pontefract Road,
Barnsley, South Yorkshire, S71 1HN, England
E-mail: enquiries@pen-and-sword.co.uk
Website: www.pen-and-sword.co.uk

or

PEN AND SWORD BOOKS
1950 Lawrence Rd, Havertown, PA 19083, USA
E-mail: uspen-and-sword@casematepublishers.com
Website: www.penandswordbooks.com

FSC
www.fsc.org
MIX
Paper | Supporting responsible forestry
FSC® C013604

# Contents

## PART FIVE: SEX



## PART SIX: IT'S A SIN



## PART SEVEN: RIOT, TREASON, REBELLION, AND CONSPIRACY



## PART EIGHT: EMPIRE AND GLORY



## PART NINE: THE CULTURAL LIFE



## PART TEN: SCANDAL

# Introduction

Britain is a country whose history is defined by a thousand years of monarchy. For the most part it has been ruled by kings, but also for significant periods by queens. There was a brief interruption we know as the interregnum: twelve years of Republicanism so chaotic and so unloved that the people embraced the return of their exiled king as both a blessing and their salvation. The monarchy would not always prove so popular, of course, but it would serve as a leitmotif, the ever-present factor in any understanding of Britain's past. A past viewed through the prism of the dynasts from the early Saxon and Norman kings to the Plantagenets and the houses of Lancaster and York, the Tudors, the Stuarts and, for the purpose of this book, the four Georges who reigned between 1714 and 1830, paving the way for the Victorianism that still pervades the public consciousness today and the sunset years of Edwardian Britain that followed.

I shall seek to understand and cast light upon the lives, ambitions, events, and indeed sufferings of the Georgians, rich and the poor alike, with stories of smugglers and highwaymen, of riot and rebellion, scandal and vice, iniquity and slavery, the sleaze, the power, and the glory. In art, in politics, in war, and in everyday life. In all its stories and its truths, both great and grim, that form our history and continue to resonate with us even today, Georgian Britain will be revealed.

# Part One

# Dynasty

# Chapter 1

# The Hanoverians

'If you profess the popish religion or marry a papist, you shall be excluded.'

On 1 August 1714, Queen Anne of Great Britain and Ireland died. Her death marked not just the passing of a monarch, but also the end of a dynasty.

Poor Queen Anne: moody, dull of conversation, and with a devotion to the table that saw her weight balloon year upon year, she was little loved or admired, but her reign had been neither uneventful nor insignificant. The Act of Union with Scotland in 1707 had seen the emergence of Britain as a political entity; Anne's great general, John Churchill, had thwarted the ambitions of the French King Louis XIV to dominate the Continent of Europe; and Britain's overseas trade had increased to unprecedented levels. But her legacy was blighted by the fact she died childless and left no heir. This was not from the want of trying: Anne's seventeen pregnancies produced just one surviving son who had predeceased her. Normally this would have been a cause of great concern, but provision had already been made for just such a scenario.

The Act of Settlement of 1701 had already decided the succession by determining that no Roman Catholic nor any potential heir married to a Roman Catholic could inherit the throne. As a result, fifty-six Catholic Stuarts with a better claim to the throne were overlooked to reach the Protestant Sophia of Hanover. As the granddaughter of King James I she had the required Stuart blood, and she was understandably delighted at her elevation. But it wasn't to be. Already elderly, she died suddenly if not entirely unexpectedly aged eighty-three, just six weeks before Queen Anne herself, bequeathing her inheritance to her 54-year-old son Georg Ludwig.

The fractious Stuarts, who had sowed division, warred with their parliament, been deposed, restored, and then deposed again, were replaced at last by a branch of the family illegitimate according to some and barely recognised by most. Henceforth, the British Royal family would no longer be English or Scottish. It would be German.

The barge carrying Britain's new Hanoverian king arrived late at Greenwich and was almost missed in the swirling fog that had descended, with many who had turned out to greet him having long since departed. Even so, a great fanfare was made of his arrival, and it had to be, for the nation was split. George was the choice of the Whigs, the commercial class that dominated in parliament, while many crown and sceptre Tories still advocated for the Catholic James Edward Francis Stuart, the Old Pretender. It was a political divide mirrored in society as a whole: rebellion was coming, and everyone knew it. But for now, the consensus was for stability and as physically unimpressive as he was, being of medium height, thickset, unsmiling and by no means handsome or dashing, George was certainly stable. Indeed, he was calm, sober, and modest to an extreme. He may have lacked the grandeur of the Stuarts, but his simple ways soon led to ridicule. Known as 'The Turnip' because of his apparent fondness for the vegetable and his desire to grow them in St James' Park, he was also mocked for his two mistresses, Ehrengard and Charlotte, one fat and the other less so, both German. His constant companions, his two Mohammedan manservants Mustapha and Mahomet, led to nods and winks of the suggestive kind, but at least added an element of the exotic to a king who avoided the royal court in favour of his private chambers where he dined alone on good German fare prepared by his good German cook.

George was by nature a shy man, a characteristic often mistaken for stupidity. His poor English did not help in this regard, and he communicated with his ministers in French, or in the case of Sir Robert Walpole, in Latin. Mary, the wife of Edward Montague, a Treasury official who met often with the King, recorded her impressions of the new monarch:

> In private life he would have been called an honest blockhead; and the fortune that made him King added nothing to his happiness and only prejudiced his honesty and shortened his days. No man was ever freer of ambition; he loved money, but loved to keep his own, while not being rapacious of other men's.

It was true that George had little love for his new realm: he missed the landscape of his homeland, and returned to Hanover as often as he could, though he required parliamentary approval to do so. However, as uncharismatic as he was, he was not free of scandal.

George's wife, Sophia Dorothea, had been having an affair with the Swedish Count Philip Christoph von Konigsmarck. George could not have cared less: the marriage was only ever one of convenience and had in any case long since soured, but when the affair became public the humiliation was too much to bear. The scandal only worsened when the count mysteriously disappeared, never to be seen again, fuelling rumours of his murder. George was quick to act: he divorced his wife and charged her with abandonment. Found guilty in a court of law, she was confined in Ahlden Castle where she was to stay for the remaining thirty-two years of her life. She was also barred from seeing her son, the future George II. He would never forgive his father for his cruelty toward his mother, and their estrangement would only increase over time. When they met, as they must, their time together was short and the words exchanged often harsh and threatening.

The inevitable rebellion we touched upon earlier came just over a year after George I inherited the crown in September 1715, when the Jacobites in Scotland rose in support of the Stuart claimant to the throne. Riots followed in many English towns, but the king neither panicked nor made any plans to flee. If the Hanoverians shared anything other than a mutual loathing for one another it was a stubborn streak, and George was undoubtedly a brave man, having served with distinction at the Siege of Vienna.

The rebellion, at first thought to be serious, soon fizzled out following an indecisive if bloody encounter at Sheriffmuir. The Old Pretender, who had arrived too late to participate, surveyed the landscape, breathed deeply of the Highland air, and then fled back to France complaining of nosebleeds.

The comparative merits of the two men convinced most that the Hanoverian succession and the dullard it had installed may have been a good thing for England after all.

# Part Two

# The People

The Georgians were a liberated people, the children of the Restoration generation, freed from the moral strictures of the Puritan divines and the hard yards required to satisfy the commonwealth men of previous years, and they behaved in a manner which reflected their new-found freedom. A gay abandon prevailed, sometimes bawdy indeed, a word often associated with the Georgians, rumbustious even.

This can be seen in the novels of Henry Fielding, Samuel Richardson, and Laurence Stern; Hogarth's 'The Rake's Progress', and John Gay's *Beggar's Opera*. The Georgians were present at the birth of satire and revelled in seeing their betters lampooned in the illustrations of James Gilray and George Cruickshank. But where freedom prevails so also lurks the devil, haunting both the corridors of power and the more labyrinthine recesses of the human soul. This was often manifest in a violent reality where the punishments were harsh and often administered arbitrarily. For freedom there is always a price to pay.

# Chapter 1

# Social Class

> 'View the large, and once most beautiful, churches; see the parson's house, large, and in the midst of pleasure gardens; and then look at the miserable sheds in which the labourers reside! Look at these hovels, made of mud and straw; bits of glass, or of old off-cast windows, without frames or hinges, frequently, but merely stuck in the mud wall. Enter them, and look at the bits of chairs or stools; the wretched boards tacked together, to serve for a table; the floor of pebble, broken brick, or of the bare ground; look at the thing called a bed; and survey the rags on the backs of the wretched inhabitants; and then wonder if you can, that the jails and dungeons and treadmills increase...'

Such scenes were not uncommon in Georgian Britain. Life was brutal. You would have been cold and wet much of the time with no means of keeping warm other than the clothes on your back and that provided by the naked flame. Your stomach was often empty. Your physical ailments went untreated. But this tells only half the story.

For most the poverty was grinding and absolute, but the rich were very rich indeed, and though people may have had greater freedom of action than in previous years, it was never a politically sanctioned liberty. Rather it was the consequence of the 180 peers and 1,500 gentry who ran the country not wanting anything to do with the lower classes other than have them tend to their needs. For the most part, the rich viewed the poor as the enemy within, to be spied upon and schooled with a rod of iron. Servants, for example, were expected to remain silent in the presence of their masters unless otherwise directed. Parallel corridors and stairways were constructed in homes to ensure the different classes should not by chance encounter one another.

The poor, it was widely held, could not be trusted: they were to be feared. Those with servants had to protect themselves against them, so the cutlery was counted, the pantry audited, the best port and brandy locked away. Likewise, the meat produced on the rich man's estate remained on the rich man's estate and, as a defence against poachers, man-traps littered the landscape and gamekeepers would shoot to kill.

The two separate classes rarely communicated, it seemed, and the gulf between rich and poor was as great as it had been in medieval times, perhaps more so since the end of serfdom had removed the sense of responsibility the nobility and wealthier landowners might have felt towards their tenants and the labourers who worked the land. Likewise, the Anglican Church and its clergy, once thought a unifying force in society, was now seen by many to be less the 'Good Shepherd' than a client of the wealthy.

# Chapter 2

# Where they Lived

The homes of the rich, the aristocratic, and the ennobled, simple in style but grand and imposing nonetheless, dominated the skyline of many a country estate. They stood majestic at the end of long gravel pathways in perfectly landscaped gardens, far removed from the problems of the day, and uncluttered by the presence of commoners. Indeed, at Houghton Hall in Norfolk, Sir Robert Walpole had a nearby village dismantled brick-by-brick and moved further away because it spoiled the view from his drawing room.

In an age of splendour and display, the optics of illusion were ever paramount, and here in their pleasure domes the rich dined on the best food and imbibed the finest wines, served to them by liveried servants on silver platters and from cut-glass decanters. As cold and uninviting as the cavernous mausoleums to self-gratification might be, there would be a fire in every room, drapes at every window, and chandeliers hung from ornamented and painted ceilings. The rich were the exception, of course.

Most houses, by contrast, were very basic indeed – still wattle and daub in more remote rural areas – and their quality varied according to geography, with local materials used to build local homes. Sparsely furnished and rarely decorated, fine porcelain and glazed marble imported from Italy were not for everyone. The walls were often damp and the space for windows not covered by glass but by a curtain, a blanket, or simply boarded up. There was no heating other than a single fire if the means to light one were available. There was no plumbing, no running water, no flushing toilet. Open sewers ran in the streets, where all waste, human and animal, was deposited. Water for drinking and washing was brought in a bucket from the nearest street pump, often drawn from the same river the sewers ran into. These pumps were the primary source of the typhoid and cholera epidemics that swept the country in the early Victorian period. The rubbish, rotting food and faecal matter strewn in the streets attracted vermin, which only helped to spread disease.

The household toilet was the chamber pot, disposed of in the street often to the detriment of an unsuspecting passer-by. The requirement to relieve oneself was a somewhat more civilised activity in the rich man's house, where a room containing a commode would be set aside and the commode would later be emptied by servants. Or, in the homes of the better-off dung men would be paid to collect the daily waste, which might later be used as fertiliser, an early form of recycling.

In the countryside toilets were often little more than a hole in the ground to be squatted over, sometimes provided with a suitably holed bench. These were considered a public amenity. Waste that collected and piled up was often burned, and the smell of the dung heap was everywhere.

# Chapter 3

# Health and Hygiene

In Georgian Britain there was no healthcare as such, other than traditional remedies for malady, herbal medicines purchased from an apothecary, old wives' tales, and taking to one's bed. Few could afford a physician, and even if you could treatments had barely moved on since the time of Hippocrates and Galen: of humors, leeching, bleeding, and the avoidance of bad odours. There had been some medical advances, of course: Edward Jenner's vaccination against smallpox in 1796, Humphrey Davy's work on anaesthetics in 1800, and much work had been done on human anatomy, but there was still no understanding of germs as the root cause of disease. As a result, illness was commonplace, particularly the fever, known as ague, brought on by damp living conditions, skin inflammations, scarring, and gastric problems. Dentistry was in its infancy, and it was often the case that the barber who cut your hair would also be the man who pulled your teeth. If he was willing to do so and had the required pliers.

There was no profession of nursing or midwifery: babies were delivered by a woman's female relatives or neighbours. Sometimes they were not delivered at all, and 1 in 4 pregnant women would eventually die in childbirth.

There were hospitals: the Royal London was founded in 1740 and St Bartholemew's had been in existence since 1123, but the care provided was often rudimentary at best and they were seen less as a place to be healed than a place to die.

Keeping clean was always problematic. Urine remained the most effective stain-remover and many still believed that it was more important to keep one's clothes clean than it was one's body. Soaking in water was thought to allow disease to enter the body via any cuts or abrasions on the skin. So firmly held was this view that the nobility was the last sector of society to have plumbing installed in homes. Nonetheless, water remained the most effective means to wash away the dirt. So, the better off would body and face wash daily using a basin and a sponge, but baths were only taken once or twice a month. The poor would do likewise, when the opportunity allowed.

Well-to-do women spent many hours at their toilette, sponge-bathing, hair grooming, and applying scents. Cosmetics remained rudimentary with a mixture of powdered chalk, lead, mercury, egg white and vinegar used to produce a fashionably pale complexion. Animal fats mashed with herbs and the petals of flowers produced a lipstick that could be perfumed using aromatic oils. Starch mixed with a stewed dark wood produced a rouge. Shampoo was made with shavings of soap mixed with warm water. Hair oils were regularly used, while a common face cream was made with white wax, almond oil, and spermaceti, the popular wax extracted from the head cavity of the sperm whale.

Men, of course, appreciated a woman's efforts to look nice, but the authorities frowned on the use of cosmetics as a form of deceit, hiding the real appearance behind paints and the mask of beauty to seduce young men and ensnare husbands. In 1770, the government passed a law that stipulated that:

> Virgins, maids, or widows found imposing on, seducing, or betraying into matrimony by virtue of scents, paints, cosmetic washes, false hair, or bolstered hips shall incur the penalty of the law now in force against witchcraft.

The law was largely ignored.

Some apothecaries would produce toothpaste of sorts: a mixture of gunpowder and alum being recommended by some. If such a recipe wasn't available then a toothpick, warm water, and a sponge to scrub one's gums with would do.

Both men and women wore powdered wigs, but this wasn't just a fashion statement. Many kept their own real hair short to avoid lice.

# Chapter 4

# What they Ate

As we have already seen, the rich dined well on the finest meats and turtle soup, even if much of the pleasure in doing so was lost in delivery from kitchen, to table, to plate. The food was rarely served hot, was lukewarm at best, and was often eaten cold. It was also a heavy diet with fewer vegetables than one might imagine. Many still thought them unhealthy and they were often pickled or stewed before being eaten. The main course of leg of lamb or roast beef was followed by rich, often fruit-based pastries and cakes, a diet not given to produce agility of mind or body. Liquorice was extremely popular as an aid to digestion, as was a spoonful of sugar with wine or brandy. Even so, despite an extreme tendency towards the bilious, a fondness for port and the ever-present prospect of gout that resulted, rich Georgians were at least never subject to the same threat of food poisoning as the poor.

The staple diet of the majority in England and Wales was bread and cheese. Indeed, the cost of bread would be the great arbiter of poverty in England. For the rural poor the Enclosure Acts had removed much of the common land used for grazing animals, making starvation a real possibility. This was particularly true for landless labourers who, poorly paid and with their work seasonal, had been reliant upon the few livestock they possessed to see them through the lean months. The Enclosures had a devastating impact, but in turn increased the popularity of the potato, previously derided and frowned upon because of its association with the peasant Irish. For the Georgian rural poor struggling to survive day-by-day, a potato patch could quite literally be life-saving.

Each region of the country had its own specialities of course: Cornish pasties in the West Country, jellied eels in London. In Scotland the staple diet was porridge, or oatmeal mixed with milk or warm water and seasoned with salt. In much of Ireland, as we have seen, the potato was the main staple, though over-reliance on a single crop would prove catastrophic in the future when that crop failed.

Food was more readily available in towns than it was in the country, though what the townsfolk were actually eating was often a subject of conjecture. The adulteration of food, though strictly illegal, was widespread. Bread was regularly contaminated with alum and anything else that could be suitably crushed to add bulk and texture. Copper was often found to have been added to pickles to provide colour, lead was found in mustard, and chalk in cheese and butter. Around 45 per cent of the tea sold contained large amounts of dirt and sand; likewise, coffee regularly had acorns and sawdust added. Foods were even infused with hallucinogens, while opium was used to water down beer.

Meat remained the most popular food. In the countryside this was often rabbit, illicitly obtained from a rich man's estate. In the towns people bought scraps of meat, most often offal, and not always of the best quality: cow's ears, sheep's trotters, mutton, tripe, and faggots. It has been estimated that as much as half of the meat eaten in London, for example, was from diseased animals or contained traces of human and animal excrement. Meat was also rarely covered and, in the summer, would be exposed to many hours in direct sunlight.

With no means of preservation other than a larder of sorts people shopped daily for their food, but the poor person's pennyworth did not go far. As a result, pies were immensely popular, though what went into them was best not spoken about.

Unsurprisingly, food poisoning was greatly feared and digestive pain a constant companion.

# Chapter 5

# What to Wear

For more detail on fashion see the chapter on Georgian style, but we will begin here with a brief overview.

When it came to clothing, the poor could only hope to ape their betters and there were few opportunities to dress to impress: even owning a change of clothes at all was an advantage. Nonetheless, the poor could still have a sense of style, even if diminished circumstances reduced this to a buckle on his shoes allowing a man to present himself with a sense of swagger, or a woman treasuring a silk ribbon or a colourful bonnet that was both a luxury and a prized possession.

As spare and threadbare as it later became, at least the quality of clothing had improved by Georgian times with the increased availability of cheap cotton from India and North America. Linen now replaced heavy woollen clothing that was too hot in summer and impossible to dry in winter. However, linen tore easily, ensuring that 'make do and mend' became the order of the day. It is perhaps indicative of the poverty of the time that in Charles Dickens's novel *Oliver Twist*, written in 1837, the target of Fagin's gang of street urchins and pickpockets was primarily the silk handkerchiefs of the well-dressed. Dickens, of course, had grown into adulthood during the reign of George IV.

In the countryside the mode of dress was more uniform, with most rural labourers wearing a straw hat, knee-length smock and boots. Trousers were rarely worn.

Women, both rich and poor, wore loose fitting dresses designed to display ample bosom with undergarments an optional extra. The restrictive intricacies of multiple layers, over-elaborate corsetry, and hoop skirts were for an era still to come. For now, it was the men who sacrificed for fashion with their ball-busting tight breeches, up to the chin wraparound neckerchiefs, and leather boots so tight they were difficult to put on and almost impossible to remove.

# Chapter 6

# How they Played

'The devil makes work for idle hands' and with no radio or television to distract them, for the Georgians the hours passed slowly, and the nights were long. The need for amusements was paramount and so, along with those hardy perennials of sex and alcohol, this was the era of board and parlour games.

The women of wealthy families, for whom any physical activity was frowned upon as unbecoming, were particularly fond of such games. They might by day be found at their crochet, reading, or strolling through a country garden, but at night they made for the drawing room to play a hand of bridge or a game of backgammon, or if men were present a turn of blind man's buff or charades.

The men, of course, had no such restrictions on their activities. Shooting, fox-hunting and hare-coursing were favoured pursuits, with horse-racing, the sport of kings, at its pinnacle. A vigorous outdoor life was soothed at night with a game of billiards and a hearty meal washed down with brandy and port. This thin veneer of gentility distracted from the bloodlust of their daily activities.

No such veneer disguised the bloodcurdling activities of the poor: dog-fighting, cock-fighting, bear-baiting and bare-knuckle pugilism were the order of the day, though like their wealthier brethren the desire to enact violence and see blood was less a draw than the opportunity to gamble on any outcome, the great obsession that seemed to affect all, whether it be ha'pennies bet on the draw of a card, or thousands of guineas wagered on the Oaks at Goodwood.

The rough and tumble of everyday Georgian life was reflected in the sports the Georgians played, such as football or versions of it: a festival of wrestling, kicking, hair-pulling and eye-gouging, with a ball of sorts.

Cards remained the most popular pastime with rich and poor alike; whether it was played at a table in a darkened room lit by a single lamp or candle that emitted barely enough light to see the other players faces, or illuminated beneath a chandelier shining bright. Many a dark winter's night was whiled away playing a game of loo or whist or cribbage (the only game that could be legally gambled on in taverns).

Having been banned during the Commonwealth the theatre had long since become popular once more, especially in the provinces, and audience participation was no less enthusiastic than it had been in Shakespeare's day. Audience members might well cheer to the rafters a performance they liked, but they were just as inclined to display their displeasure through heckling, bad language, barely veiled threats and rotten vegetables. The well-dressed and the well-heeled were advised to wear large hats, as with no 'facilities' to speak in the theatre, those who could afford standing room only took great delight in relieving themselves on their betters in the stalls below. Revenge takes all forms.

However, among this wide range of amusements nothing was as well received and as much loved as music and dancing. The wealthy might appreciate the elegance and formalities of the ballroom, the subtleties of a finely tuned harp, and a little early evening chamber music, but for most music had to be enjoyed where it could be found and heard: the man with a fiddle, the piccolo player on the street. People flocked to the sound, they would sing along, and the dancing would be spontaneous. A fine voice was always appreciated, and a song rendered beautifully could silence a crowd then just as it does today.

At a time when existence could be perilous, uncertain, and often brief, people nevertheless had a lust for life and a determination to enjoy it, so a travelling circus always drew a crowd, as did a country fair or a public hanging. It took little encouragement for a crowd to gather, though whether the outcome would be a night of revelry and dancing, or a public riot, always remained to be seen.

# Chapter 7

# How they Died

'The curfew tolls the knell of parting day
The lowing herd wind slowly o'er the lea,
The ploughman homeward plods his weary way,
And leaves the world to darkness and to me.'

So wrote Thomas Grey in his 'Elegy Written in a Country Churchyard' of 1750, the most celebrated poem of the Georgian era and one of the most admired in the entire English literary canon. His musings upon death, memory, and the obscurity of the common man in life and in his passing struck a chord in an age ill-considered as a time of reflection; but death is never absent from life and for the Georgians it was as visible as it had been since the times of plague. Corpses were a common sight on the streets of British towns and cities and in the ditches that ran alongside country lanes. But familiarity with death did not lessen the grief of those affected by it.

There were rules regarding a proper mourning, but the elaborate rituals of the Victorians, who engaged in death with an intensity that we find uncomfortable today, had not yet been established. Life was short. No man or woman could expect to live to middle age, and almost one in four children would be dead before the age of five. How people were mourned varied greatly and the etiquette in place was rarely adhered to unless the deceased had been a prominent figure.

The mourning of a loved one then was brief, the raising of a glass in celebration of a life now departed, rather than the widow's veil, the drawn curtains, and endless meanderings on loss and remorse. Black remained the colour of mourning, but as the author Jonathan Swift noted, 'Black clothes are but seldom accompanied with a sorrowful countenance.' A vigorous and energetic people, the Georgians had little time for self-indulgent self-mortification.

# Part Three

# Crime and Punishment

# Chapter 1

# Who Governed?

Georgian England, which is best remembered now as a time of gentility and refinement, was also notorious for the brutality of its judicial system. During the period more than 200 crimes on the statute book carried the death penalty, imprisonment for debt was commonplace, and public floggings and executions were a popular source of entertainment.

After all, it was not the duty of the Government to improve the life of the people, and it had no desire to do so. It was however expected to protect the land and property of the lawmakers themselves, the wealthy 3 percent of the population who were permitted to vote in elections, even though they were unlikely to be the victim of crime unless it was the pickpocket on the street, the robber on the highway or from poaching on the rich man's estate.

The true beneficiaries of the draconian laws were the merchants, shop-owners and innkeepers, who along with the poor were always more vulnerable to being the victims of crime, but this was a by-product of the system and not the intention of those who made the law.

The man most responsible for the shaping of Georgian England was Robert Walpole. He was born near Houghton in Norfolk on 26 August 1676, the son of a prominent Whig politician, who upon his father's death in January 1701 was elected as Member of Parliament for his father's old constituency of Castle Rising.

British politics in the eighteenth century reflected a society divided between the monarchy-supporting landed aristocracy and the rapidly expanding commercial class that sought the primacy of parliament in all things, and it was a fraught arena where tensions often ran high.

The Tories and the Whigs were not political parties as we would understand them today, but rather factions who formed alliances to best serve their own interests. It was no friendly rivalry. They were two warring camps, each willing to take up the cudgel if required, and with their mutual enmity reflected in the names they called one another: a Tory was an Irish bandit or thief, while a Whig was a Scottish rebel or Presbyterian fanatic.

The fact that elections were held every three years guaranteed a febrile atmosphere, with members of the different factions meeting in their own coffee houses to conspire with one another and plot their opponents' downfall.

Political meetings were violent affairs, graft and corruption were commonplace, votes and constituency seats were bought and sold and the behaviour at hustings would often border on riotous assembly. Yet this was a world in which Robert Walpole, the great manipulator – not to say enabler – would thrive and prosper.

Walpole's connections ensured that he soon acquired high political office, and he quickly proved himself an able administrator, earning a reputation for probity at a time when such a thing in politics was rare, despite the fact that he had been briefly imprisoned for embezzlement in 1712.

Having gained the favour of King George I, just as he would later with his son George II, Walpole began to rise through the government ranks, but his ambition was a secret to no one, and he was hated by the Tories, who time and again tried to discredit him and have him impeached.

Walpole appeared impervious to criticism, however, and his reputation soared further following the fiasco of the South Sea Bubble. The South Sea Company had been formed in 1711 as a joint-stock enterprise which, through the sale of bonds, would purchase the national debt, but it was in fact no more than a get-rich-quick scheme underpinned by inflated promises of vast profits. The Company had been granted a monopoly on trade with South America, but Britain was at the time at war with Spain, meaning there was little real trade to be had, a fact seemingly overlooked by most investors.

The rich flocked to buy shares, but by 1720 it was apparent that the South Sea Company was an empty shell and the rush to sell shares caused it to crash spectacularly. Although Walpole had also invested heavily, he had earlier been advised to sell his shares. Even so, he tried to reinvest, but his purchase of further shares was delayed in the mail and did not arrive in time. This was to prove a stroke of good fortune both financially and, more significantly, politically: coupled with a few minor criticisms he had made of the company's behaviour in the House of Commons, it appeared to many that he'd had the foresight to see the crash coming. Nothing could have been further from the truth, but this stroke of luck provided him with a reputation for financial rectitude at a time when others who should have known better had allowed their greed to overrule their common sense.

The king now turned to Walpole to help the government out of the financial mess it found itself in, and he seized the opportunity with aplomb.

Walpole was quick to smooth things over, making a series of emollient and reassuring speeches in the House of Commons and confiscating the estates of the company's directors to pay off those worst hit financially in the crisis. He also deflected criticism away from the king, who as governor of the company was heavily implicated in its wrongdoings. For this both the king and his successor George II would be eternally grateful.

Appointed to the position of First Lord of the Treasury alongside several other high offices, Walpole became indispensable to the king and effectively Britain's first Prime Minister. He was to remain in position for the next fifteen years. This was the beginning of the 'Whig Supremacy' and Walpole was to refashion Georgian England in his own image: a country of both conspicuous wealth and extreme poverty, of unapologetic self-interest and punitive laws.

Walpole, or Cock Robin as he was known, not always with affection, secured his own position by accumulating a vast array of patronage, ensuring that people who would be his men in parliament were elected in so-called 'rotten boroughs'. Aware that he could break as well as make political careers where bribery didn't serve his purposes, he wasn't averse to a little intimidation. As a last resort he could always turn to the king for support.

Walpole's policy would be to maintain the status quo by appealing to the naked self-interest of those who mattered. He adopted a policy of peace, avoiding ruinously expensive wars, kept taxes low, especially those on land, and introduced laws that would protect property, game, and livestock.

Thus, the rich could sit back and enjoy their wealth, comfortable in the knowledge that they were safe from robbery, revolution and foreign invasion. As long as the calm waters of conspicuous self-indulgence and display remained undisturbed, then all was well in Georgian England.

It would prove, for the time being at least, a winning formula.

# Chapter 2

# Prison

The most potent symbol of Walpole's England was the debtor's prison. Every major city had at least one and there were seven in London alone, the most notorious of which were the Fleet Prison in Farringdon Street and the Marshalsea Prison at Southwark. These prisons were government owned but privately managed and were run for profit.

For example, in 1728 Thomas Bambridge purchased the Letters of Patent to run the Fleet Prison as its warden for £5,000, and, like most wardens, he immediately divided the prisoners into those who could pay for their keep and those who could not. Indeed, Bambridge was to become particularly notorious for extorting money from his inmates, even manacling them on occasions until his demands were met.

It was possible to be imprisoned for a debt as little as £2 and incarceration would often come as the result of a request from the creditor. While a debtor was in prison the interest on their debt would continue to accrue, and release would only come after a financial arrangement had been made for repayment of the debt or the creditor relented. With no specific time to be served, a prisoner could be wrangling for his release ad nauseam.

For those able to pay, imprisonment would be less onerous and, depending on how much money they had, a prisoner might get a cell to themselves with a bed, and be able to purchase food and beer that was often brewed on the premises. Prisoners could receive visits from their family if they were not already imprisoned with them, which sometimes happened. The Fleet Prison even permitted prisoners to live within a short distance of the confines of the prison itself, a practice known as the 'Liberty of the Rules'.

If you were unable to pay for your keep then you would be left to rot in the squalor of the common cells: damp, windowless and rat-infested rooms situated on the ground floor where petty criminals were confined. They were forced to sleep on a bare floor strewn with straw, fed on gruel twice a day, and with nowhere to urinate or defecate disease was rife and life expectancy short.

The 'Bloody Code', as it was to become known, meant that offences ranging from poaching, the theft of a loaf of bread and sheep-stealing through to murder and treason carried the death penalty. It was harsh in the extreme, as were the penalties for those crimes that did not carry the ultimate sanction, such as the pillory, being publicly whipped, branded with hot irons and transportation to the colonies as an indentured slave.

Despite the many laws that made up the statute book there were few formal structures in place with which to enforce them. There was no police force at this time, so every parish was obliged to have at least a constable, but these were unpaid volunteers often concerned only with the status their position brought them rather than the actual enforcement of the law.

In London and other major cities there were paid watchmen: these were often elderly ex-soldiers who patrolled the streets at night and at the top of every hour they would ring a bell, announce the time and cry 'All is well'. Though they were much maligned at the time, watchmen did play a role in keeping the streets safe at night and provided reassurance if nothing else.

# Chapter 3

# Bow Street Runners

In 1749 the author Henry Fielding, who had been appointed Chief Magistrate for London along with his brother John, founded the Bow Street Runners. They largely replaced the 'Thief Takers', men often recruited from among the criminal underworld who would investigate crimes and arrest people for a fee. This had always been an unsatisfactory arrangement to say the least, as Thief Takers were very often involved in crimes themselves and were merely turning in their associates for money.

The new Bow Street Runners did not serve as policemen as we would now understand them. They did not attend the scene of a crime, patrol the streets at night or make themselves available for emergencies. They did, however, serve writs and make arrests on the authority of the Chief Magistrate, travelling the length and breadth of the country to do so, and they were well-rewarded, being paid a guinea a week along with a bonus for every arrest that led to a conviction. But even armed as they were with pistol, sword, and club it was not a job for the faint-hearted.

With no rules of behaviour to guide or restrain them the Bow Street Runners were notorious for their brutality and soon rose in number from six officers operating around the Covent Garden area of London to a force of almost seventy, with the addition, from 1768, of a horse patrol known as Redbreasts (from the colour of their tunics), formed to tackle the scourge of highway robbery. But feared as they were, their presence was never so widespread as to serve as a meaningful deterrent.

Justice was administered by local magistrates who were invariably drawn from among the wealthiest of any parish. They were unpaid and often found their work burdensome and time-consuming. Also, there was no oversight of their activities and they were not necessarily averse to acting maliciously or taking bribes. Indeed, the gothic novelist Horace Walpole, the son of Robert, remarked of the magistrates in London: '*The greatest criminals of this town are the officers of justice.*'

More serious crimes, such as burglary, murder and treason, would be tried before the Quarterly Assizes and in London at Newgate, later to become the Old Bailey. Unlike trials for petty crime, more serious offences were tried before a jury of the accused person's peers. It was the norm for such cases to be dealt with quickly, particularly as it was rare for there to be a defence barrister present, expensive as they were, and none was provided by the State. Also, the presumption on the part of the magistrates was always that the defendant was guilty. The fact that the courtroom itself would be liberally sprinkled with fresh-smelling herbs and flowers to mask the smell of the filthy and unwashed prisoners was indicative of the attitude of those dispensing justice towards those on the receiving end of their verdicts.

A guilty verdict at the Quarterly Assizes would invariably carry the death penalty and such trials were well-attended and raucous affairs. The crowd would heckle and jeer throughout, but silence would descend upon the courtroom as the judge placed the black cap upon his head and passed the sentence of death:

> Prisoner at the bar, it is now my painful duty to pronounce the awful sentence of the law which must follow the verdict that has just been recorded, that you be taken to the place of execution there to be hanged by the neck until you are dead, and may the Lord have mercy on your sinful soul.

# Chapter 4

# The Gallows

Executions were public and in London they were carried out at Tyburn, where they were occasions for a social gathering in an atmosphere akin to that of a fairground, as thousands of people gathered in the field where the gallows were located, stalls were set up and entertainments were underway. Others lined the streets of the three-mile journey of the condemned man from his place of incarceration to his place of execution.

Carried on a cart, where he would be sat upon his own coffin, and accompanied by the sheriff, a chaplain and an armed escort, the condemned prisoner was, for a short period at least, the centre of attention. Sometimes, as the cart passed a tavern, the landlord would offer the prisoner a last drink, to which the sheriff would invariably reply: 'Not for him, he's on the wagon.'

There was a celebratory feel to the day of an execution, with music, dancing, food aplenty, and many people drunk on cheap alcohol. As in the courtroom, however, once the condemned man mounted the gallows the crowd would fall silent to hear the chaplain's last words:

> You have been adjudged by the laws of this country unworthy any longer to live, unworthy to walk this earth, unworthy to breathe its air, and that no further good to mankind can be expected from you, only the example of your death to warn others in the future, and may God have mercy on your soul.

The common people knew full well that the justice system was not there to serve them, as a popular saying of the time testifies: 'The laws grind the poor, and the rich make the law.'

As a result, the more notorious a criminal, no matter how brutal, the more likely he was to be treated as a folk hero in the tradition of Robin Hood, with highwaymen such as Dick Turpin, Claude Vall and Sixteen String Jack, who intercepted and robbed the stagecoaches of the rich, particularly admired, making them the celebrities of their day. In 1774, when the famous highwayman John Rann was found not guilty of robbery,

The Last Scene, George Cruickshank (1839). (Public Domain via Wikimedia Commons)

thousands of people who had gathered outside cheered and carried him aloft from the court; but by far the most popular anti-hero was a 22-year-old apprentice carpenter whose name became synonymous with bad deeds and getting away with it.

# Chapter 5

# The Elusive Jack Sheppard

Five years into his apprenticeship, young Jack had proven to be both a diligent worker and a quick learner when, encouraged by the other apprentices, he began to frequent the Black Lion Tavern in Drury Lane, a popular haunt of the local criminal underworld. Here, along with his newly acquired taste for alcohol, he made the acquaintance of local gang leader, Joseph 'Blueskin' Blake, who soon taught him that there was easier money to be made in crime than there was in having to work for a living. Jack concurred and quickly progressed from petty theft and pickpocketing to burglary.

Arrested on numerous occasions, his increasingly spectacular prison escapes made him a popular hero. Time and again he absconded from Newgate, Bridewell and elsewhere, either by sawing through the bars of his cell or lowering himself from prison walls on knotted bedsheets. On one memorable occasion he walked out through the prison's main entrance dressed as a woman.

In prison once more, and sentenced to hang, there was an immediate clamour for Jack's sentence to be commuted to something less severe: transportation perhaps, but when he declined to inform on his associates, on the promise of leniency if he did so, the sentence was confirmed. Nonetheless he insisted he would never hang, and promised to escape on the day of his execution, but the pocketknife he always carried for cutting and lock picking was discovered. Undeterred, Jack declared he had another plan. He remained supremely confident, even boasting of his forthcoming escape and calling upon the public to come and witness it. The people expected him to be as good as his word.

The always smiling and cheerful Jack Sheppard, who was only 5ft 2in and weighed barely 100 pounds, firmly believed that as the cart was wheeled away to leave him hanging, he would not be heavy enough for the noose to break his neck, so he had arranged for his friends to cut him down and take him to a doctor to be revived.

On the day of his execution, 24 January 1724, more than 200,000 people turned out to see Jack Sheppard hang – or escape?

Jack Sheppard,
James Thornhill (1724).
(National Portrait Gallery)

On his journey to the gallows Sheppard joined in the celebratory mood, revelling in the banter and urging on the crowd. He even persuaded the sheriff to stop off at the City of Oxford Tavern so he could down a pint of ale.

Even as Jack stood beneath the gallows with his neck in the noose, he continued to play to a crowd that truly expected him to escape, but this time there was to be no such derring-do. As the cart was pulled away from beneath his feet, the raucous crowd descended into a hushed silence as they watched his body squirm and twitch. There was to be no escape this time and Jack dangled from the rope for a full 15 minutes as he endured the agonies of slow strangulation.

When Jack's body was at last cut down the crowd surged forward to grab souvenirs, pulling out his hair, cutting off his fingers and gouging out his eyes. His friends, who had planned to rescue him before death's deadly embrace took hold, never even got close to retrieving his lifeless corpse.

Such had been the popularity of the notorious Jack Sheppard that newspapers were forbidden to write of his exploits and theatres were banned from using his name for the next forty years.

# Chapter 6

# Mother's Ruin

London was the largest city in the world, with a population of over 800,000 and growing all the time. It was a place like no other, with more than 50,000 shops, taverns, restaurants, coffee houses and brothels, where every need and desire could be catered for: a place of the most outlandish display and the grimmest squalor.

The many iniquities of London, including vice, violence, and disease, were vividly captured in the paintings and lithographs of the artist William Hogarth, and no problem was more evident, or indeed more public, than that of drunkenness. Indeed, by the 1720s London was quite literally awash with beer and gin, or 'mother's ruin', as it was known.

Beer, or ale, had long been imbibed in great amounts as an alternative to water, which was thought unsafe, but the craze for gin had caught on in the 1690s following its importation from the Netherlands, and within a

Beer Street and Gin Lane, William Hogarth (1751), Old Artworks. (Public Domain via Wikimedia Commons)

decade the distilleries producing it were cropping up not just in London but throughout the country. Of the 15,000 drinking establishments in London alone more than half were gin palaces. By 1743 it is estimated that the English were drinking up to 10 litres of gin per head of population a year.

Drunkenness had become a common feature on the streets of all England's major cities and with it a corresponding rise in the crime rate, while the number of abandoned children that thronged the streets and dead babies that littered the gutters had become a national disgrace. But attempts to stamp out the craze for gin found little success.

The Gin Act of 1736, which priced it at 20 shillings a gallon and required a licence to sell it at a fee of £50 per annum, provoked disturbances so violent that they led to the Act being repealed in 1742. A further attempt to curtail the production and distribution of gin the following year led to the 'Gin Riots' that left many dead and caused widespread destruction throughout London.

The introduction of a series of more moderate measures brought about a decline in the consumption of gin. Drunkenness remained a common sight on the streets of Britain, but by the mid-1750s gin was no longer considered its root cause. Mother's ruin had been banished to the margins, as had Robert Walpole, the man who had done so much to forge Georgian Britain in his own image.

By the early 1740s Walpole was no longer seen as the guardian of wealth, but as an impediment to growth and increased prosperity. People had tired of the widespread corruption that had come to mark his time in power. His policy of placating Britain's enemies abroad, once thought necessary for the maintenance of stability and continued prosperity, had since come to be seen as a national humiliation, while his increased taxes on commodities to ensure that the tax on land remained low was damaging the economy.

The growing and aspirational middle class, and even many of Walpole's natural supporters among the nobility and gentry, now saw their futures in overseas trade and the expansion of Empire, and so, with his enemies – and he had always had many – gathering in Parliament, and fearing impeachment, on 11 February 1742 he resigned, returning to his palatial home at Houghton Hall a bitter and resentful man. He died there he died in great splendour three years later on 18 March 1745, aged sixty-eight, a bloated caricature of himself and the country he had created.

The draconian laws that Walpole had introduced did not die with him, however. Indeed, the number of capital offences on the statute book increased and it remained possible to be hanged for impersonating a Chelsea

Pensioner, going out at night with a blackened face, damaging a turnpike, or writing a threatening letter. Most of these offences would continue to carry the death penalty late into the Victorian era, though as the decades passed they were rarely enforced.

Even so, between 1791 and 1891, long after the Bloody Codes had first been introduced, more than 10,000 people were hanged in England alone, and imprisonment for debt and debtor's prisons were not abolished until the Bankruptcy Act of 1869.

The first professional police force wasn't established until 1829 when the then Home Secretary, Sir Robert Peel, formed the Metropolitan Police to investigate crime and maintain law and order on the streets of London.

# Part Four

# Heroes and Villains

# Chapter 1

# Highwaymen (and how to survive them)

As we have seen, eighteenth-century England was a violent place and a country of extremes: great wealth but greater poverty, with politics shorn of scruple and a law without justice. Few people journeyed far from their homes, especially at night; it was not just dangerous to do so, but also difficult, with roads few and poorly maintained, and, since the Turnpike Act of 1706, increasingly expensive. Those paths that existed were less than well-trod, while the streets remained cobbled and uneven, and if there wasn't a robber lurking around every corner then people feared there was. Moreover, for most the requirement to travel meant doing so on foot as horses were expensive to feed and stable and coach travel was affordable only for the few.

In such a world pickpockets and thieves, fraudsters, and robbers on the highway – so long as they stole from the rich and regardless of whether they gave to the poor –were to be honoured.

In a brutal world and with their trademark address beloved by generations of children, *'Stand and deliver. Your money or your life'*, none was more admired than the highwayman who terrorised with impunity by night those who governed with an iron fist by day. It was not an admiration shared by their victims, however, for not to comply with their demands imperilled not only your own life, but also those of your fellow passengers. It mattered little to the highwaymen whether you lived or died: they already dwelt beneath the shadow of the noose. But it was the humiliation involved as much as the fear for one's life that troubled victims: to be stripped of your clothing and tied to a tree to be found by those you considered your social inferiors was just too great an indignity to bear.

Portrayed in popular ballad and verse as both dashing and brave, highwaymen infested the main arteries of England, making travel a perilous pursuit undertaken with trepidation and for good reason. Most highwaymen made no pretence of gallantry but were violent thugs who would kill without compunction. But there were exceptions.

Claude Du Val, William Powell Frith (1866). (Public domain via Wikimedia Commons)

The highwayman as folk hero had been established in the decades immediately preceding the Hanoverian succession by the likes of James Hind, the royalist soldier who, following the execution of King Charles I, targeted the Commonwealth men he believed to be responsible, including on one memorable occasion the Lord Protector Oliver Cromwell himself.

If Hind's daring stirred the blood of young men, then it was the gallic charm of the émigré French nobleman Claude Du Val who stole the hearts of the young ladies. Mannered and well-dressed, it was said he had dash, panache even. With pistol cocked and feathered hat in hand, he bowed with grace to both threaten and sweet talk at the same time. The men were suitably afraid, the women duly captivated, and when he was hanged ladies of substance openly wept and mourned with deep regret at his passing.

But we begin our story with the brief criminal careers of Plunkett and MacLaine.

The highwayman's life was fraught with danger, and not just for his victims. Few coach passengers travelled unarmed and the coachman himself would often carry a blunderbuss, a scattergun with a flared nozzle that fired a multitude of musket balls that could kill both a horse and its rider with a single shot. It was important then for one man to keep the passengers covered while the other deprived them of their goods and money.

Plunkett and MacLaine worked well together and created an impression that far surpassed their deeds, but it was always their intention to do so. This remained a shared ambition for two otherwise very different men.

James MacLaine was born in Ireland, the son of a Scottish Presbyterian minister, but there any nod towards sobriety ended. He was a young man on the make, gregarious and flamboyant, who openly defied his father while also burdening the old man with his many debts. Forced to marry early in the hope that the responsibility of family life would curb his behaviour, he moved to London where, having set himself up as a grocer, if in name only, he proceeded to squander his wife's inheritance on a lifestyle he believed was his by right.

William Plunkett, so unlike his partner, was an earnest but failed businessman whose penurious situation was hardly improved by his association with MacLaine, to whom he loaned money with no prospect of it ever being repaid.

It was MacLaine who suggested crime as the way out of their shared predicament, but it was Plunkett who insisted that they be gentlemen thieves. They embarked on a career as highwaymen wearing fancy clothes, their faces hidden by Venetian masks, and with the exaggerated mannerisms they believed appropriate for men of a higher station.

Operating for the most part in the wasteland that was then Hyde Park, the pair committed robbery after robbery, stopping carriages with impunity; so much so that one of their more high-profile victims, the Gothic novelist Horace Walpole, wrote: *'One is forced to travel, even at noon, as if one is going into battle.'*

The war analogy may have been a little theatrical, but for Plunkett and MacLaine there was no robbery unworthy of a dramatic gesture, and so, while MacLaine wooed the ladies with a silver-tongued charm, the more morose Plunkett stripped them and their male companions of their valuables with a grimly determined but always polite menace. Indeed, so conscious were they of their reputation as gentleman thieves that when it was reported shots had been fired at Walpole's carriage MacLaine wrote a letter of apology, along with a corresponding demand for money:

> Sir, seeing an advertisement in the papers of today of you being robbed by two highwaymen on Wednesday last in Hyde Park and during the time a pistol was fired intended or accidental obliges us to take this method of assuring you it was the latter and was designed by no means to frighten or

> hurt you for we are reduced by the misfortunes of the world to have recourse to this method of getting money. Yet we have humanity enough not to take anybody's life where there is not a necessity. We have likewise seen the advertisement offering a reward of 20 guineas for your watch and seals which are very safe and which you shall have along with your sword and the coachman's watch for 40 guineas and not a shilling less.

The missive then provided for the delivery of the money before once again burnishing the pair's image as latter-day Robin Hoods by promising to return the few pennies and cheap pocket watch they had stolen from Walpole's poor footman.

As a gesture the letter and return of goods meant little and did not deflect from their avarice, yet no matter how valuable their haul MacLaine, in particular, never failed to spend it. Residing in expensive lodgings with a wardrobe of fine clothes and a live-in mistress bought and paid for, he even then struggled to make ends meet and it was his pawning of some expensive lace that led to the pair's downfall. In attempting to sell the lace the pawnbroker offered it to the tailor who had made the waistcoat from which it had been unpicked. Aware that the waistcoat had been stolen in a robbery he reported the incident to the authorities, leading to MacLaine's arrest.

There is of course no honour among thieves and MacLaine immediately revealed Plunkett's whereabouts and declared he was willing to turn King's Evidence against him for a guarantee of immunity from prosecution. But it was the dashing MacLaine who was wanted to make an example of, not the dour Plunkett, and it was the latter not the former who would ultimately betray his friend.

Hundreds of well-wishers visited MacLaine while he was in prison awaiting trial, but popularity was to prove no defence, and he was hanged at Tyburn on 3 October 1750. William Plunkett, meanwhile, remained free to spend his ill-gotten gains and disappeared into well-earned obscurity on the other side of the Atlantic.

Plunkett and MacLaine's notoriety as highwaymen was fleeting, as was that of others such as John Nevinson, referred to as 'Swift Nicks' by the King himself, and 'Sixteen String' Jack Rann, so named for the colourful silk stripes he had elaborately sewn into his breeches. None however acquired a fame as enduring as Dick Turpin. His was a legend that grew after his death, as a result of William Ainsworth Harrison's popular 1830 novel *Rookwood,* in which he appeared as a peripheral but particularly vivid character.

Richard 'Dick' Turpin was born in the Bluebell Inn, Hempstead, in the county of Essex, in September 1705, the son of a butcher in whose trade he would follow. Indeed, it was in the fencing of stolen livestock and poached meat that he became part of the local criminal underworld.

Crime paid, or so it seemed, and it certainly provided easier money than the long hours and hard graft of butchery, and so by 1734 Dick was working not as a butcher, but as a member of the Essex Gang led by the brothers Samuel and Jeremiah Gregory. So it was not as a highwayman that Dick Turpin began his life as a career criminal, but as a burglar and street robber.

In February 1735, Turpin, along with four other members of the Essex Gang, broke into the isolated farmhouse of 70-year-old Joseph Lawrence, bound and gagged his two maidservants and tortured the old man to discover where he had hidden his money. They stripped him, beat him, roasted his bare buttocks over the open fire, and poured boiling water over his head. When he still stubbornly refused to give up his fortune a furious Turpin pistol-whipped the old man unconscious. In their frustration the gang then ransacked the house while the Gregory brothers took the women upstairs and raped them.

Later that same month the gang broke into another isolated house, this time belonging to an elderly widow, Elizabeth Shelley, whom they again brutalised before escaping with £100 in coin and her silver plate.

This is not the popular image of Dick Turpin the highwayman we have today, but the Lawrence and Shelley robberies were just two of a series of violent incidents that occurred in quick succession. Indeed, the fear they spread forced the authorities to act and, using paid informers and government spies, the gang was infiltrated and broken up, its members arrested, and in the case of the Gregory brothers, hanged. Only Dick Turpin of the dozen or so gang members escaped justice, but he was now a marked man. The Duke of Newcastle offered a substantial reward for his arrest and his description was widely circulated to the press. This appeared in the *London Gazette*:

> A butcher by trade about 26 years of age, a tall fresh coloured man very much marked with the smallpox. Lived some time ago in Whitechapel and wears a blue grey coat and natural wig.

Turpin had indeed fled to the anonymity of the teeming and smog-bound city, but he did not lie low for long before turning once more to crime, this

Highway Robbery, anonymous. (Public domain via Wikimedia Commons)

time highway robbery. It wasn't for the most part well-protected carriages he targeted, however, but lone travellers defenceless and vulnerable amid the woodland and bleak moors that still surrounded much of London. He also rarely worked alone, his most regular accomplice being Matthew King, with whom he carried out a great many robberies; but a partner in crime is not necessarily a friend, as King was soon to discover.

Having been disturbed while trying to steal some horses, King was overpowered and called upon Turpin, who was hiding nearby, to save him. However, Turpin fled. He returned soon after, drew his pistol and shot King dead. This may have been unintentional and the result of a confused mêlée, but it was convenient. After his partner's death Turpin's involvement and whereabouts remained secret. Even so, he took the precaution of moving to Epping Forest, an area he knew well. However, with a £200 reward on his head, familiarity with the place would not keep him safe. On 4 May 1737 he killed Thomas Morris, a servant to one of the keepers of the forest, who, having recognised the notorious highwayman, had attempted to apprehend him.

The cold-blooded murder of the unarmed Morris was a cowardly act, reported the length and breadth of the country. For a time Turpin was the most wanted man in England. One such report appeared in the *Gentleman's Quarterly* of June 1737:

> It having been represented to the King, that Richard Turpin did on Wednesday the 4th of May last, barbarously murder Thomas Morris, Servant to Henry Tomson, one of the Keepers of Epping Forest and commit other notorious felonies and robberies near London, his Majesty is pleased to promise his most gracious pardon to any of his accomplices, and a reward of £200 to any person or persons that shall discover him, so that he may be apprehended and convicted. He is by trade a butcher, about 5 feet and 9 inches high with a brown complexion very much marked by the smallpox, his cheek bones broad, his face thinner towards the bottom, his visage short, upright, and broad about the shoulders.

Turpin was forced to flee once more, this time in haste, and according to legend he rode his trusty mare Black Bess through the night on an epic 11-hour, 200-mile ride to York, pausing only briefly to cool her down with a mixture of water and brandy. This proved enough to keep her going, but no sooner had they reached their destination than her heart burst and, with blood pouring from her nostrils, she dropped dead of exhaustion.

This was a great story, and it almost certainly wasn't true. A similar journey had been undertaken by John Nevinson many years before when he sought an alibi for a vicious robbery committed in London by playing a game of bowls with the Mayor of York. What was true that Turpin had fled to the city where he now lived under the alias of John Palmer.

Turpin soon embarked on a crime spree across Yorkshire and the neighbouring county of Lincolnshire, teaming up with others to poach and rob, with horse theft proving particularly lucrative. However, Turpin had also taken to drinking heavily, not just at night but throughout the day, and his behaviour had become increasingly erratic as a result.

On 2 October 1738, having just returned from a hunting trip with friends the worse for wear and in a foul mood, Turpin shot dead in the street another man's expensive cockerel, in what appears to have been an act of malice. Reported to the local magistrates, John Palmer, as he was known, was arrested. He was found guilty, and despite being able to pay the fine that was imposed on him, he refused to do so, continuing to plead his innocence. As a result, he remained in detention while an investigation was undertaken into his identity. Who was this man who lived the high life in York's taverns and brothels, while seemingly having no gainful employment? He was certainly not the simple butcher he claimed to be. He was suspected of being a horse thief and rustler of sheep, but no one had yet recognised him as the notorious Dick Turpin.

Languishing in prison, Turpin was now also accused of stealing a horse. This had been a capital offence since 1545, and though it was rare for such a harsh penalty to be imposed, it might have been wise at this point for him to pay the fine. He stubbornly refused to do so and the case was scheduled to come to trial.

With no defence counsel provided for the accused, he would be expected to represent himself. Turpin was to prove a particularly poor advocate in his own defence. Indeed, it was his ham-fisted attempt to find a character witness willing to testify on his behalf that was to prove his undoing.

One of those he approached was his brother-in-law, who, not wanting to get involved, refused even to open the letter he had received, although neither did he destroy or conceal it. James Smith, who had taught the young Richard Turpin how to write and was still in contact with the family, saw the envelope and, recognising his distinctive style, wrote to the court in York to inform them that their John Palmer was in fact Dick Turpin.

The judge presiding at the trial, Sir William Chapple, was determined to pass sentence of death on John Palmer so that Turpin would hang, and as he was charged with horse theft he had the crime for which to do so. There was no need to seek further proof of Turpin's identity, or to charge him with further felonious acts, as the capital crime had already been committed. In his haste to conclude proceedings, however, Sir William allowed the trial to descend into farce with incorrect dates, doubtful eyewitness accounts and tainted evidence. Any competent defence counsel would have seen the case thrown out of court, but as Turpin had none he was duly sentenced to hang.

Hundreds of people curious to set eyes upon the notorious Dick Turpin while he was still alive visited him in jail and thousands more attended his execution to see how he died: and he did not disappoint. He bought a new frock coat and shoes for the occasion, and paid for mourners to accompany his cart as it took him through the streets of York to his place of death. He even joined in with the carnival atmosphere: '*Turpin behaved himself with amazing assurance and bowed to spectators as he passed.*'

However, for all the bravado Dick Turpin was no less fearful of imminent death than anybody else, and as he ascended the ladder to the gallows his right leg trembled so much so that he had to pause and stamp his foot to bring it under control and regain his composure. Perhaps it was because he could sense his nerve was failing him, or to avoid the short drop that guaranteed a slow strangulation, that he jumped from the scaffold with the noose around his neck. If he believed that his 'leap into eternity' would snap his neck then he was sorely mistaken. He dangled from the rope, struggling for breath, for a full five minutes before he died.

Dick Turpin's notoriety was brief, and only later was his story revived to become a legend. It was only a year after the publication of Harrison's novel that the last genuine recorded incident of *'Stand and deliver'* occurred: the day of the highwayman had passed.

The holding up of the coaches of the rich was a crime of a very specific period, and there was already nostalgia for it long before one era had evolved into another. For those who were never victims the highwayman was a folk hero, admired by many who would never dare trespass the law of their own volition. It was not the first time a criminal has been elevated to a status well beyond the meanness of his profession. Perhaps there is just something in the human condition, restrained by a common decency, that seeks validation in the activities of those who have no such qualms if they behave in a manner otherwise acceptable to polite society. So those like John Hind, who had the noble cause, Claude Du Val, who had the gallantry and charm, and Plunkett and MacLaine who had the daring, would be idolised. Yet it would fall to Dick Turpin, a man who could lay claim to none of the above, to live on in time and space and come to epitomise the highwayman as something other than a common criminal, a figure of romance.

# Chapter 2

# Smugglers (and turning a blind eye)

'If you wake at midnight and hear a horse's feet,
Don't go drawing back the blind, or looking in the street,
Them that ask no questions isn't told a lie.
Watch the wall, my darling, while the Gentlemen go by!

Five and twenty ponies,
Trotting through the dark –
Brandy for the parson,
Baccy for the clerk;
Laces for a lady, letters for a spy,
And watch the wall, my darling,
While the Gentlemen go by!'

Smugglers, George Morland (1792). (Public domain via Wikimedia Commons)

The smuggler never shared the romance of the highwayman. Maybe this was because smuggling was the work of many, that entire coastal communities relied upon them for their livelihoods, and because they terrorised those communities in which they operated. None could ignore the presence of the smuggling gangs, and none was safe from their wrath whether high born or low, whether a representative of the law or not.

No criminal enterprise in Georgian England was more lucrative than smuggling, as the customs duties imposed on goods imported from abroad were so high that evading their payment had not only become a national pastime, but the means to a fortune. Items such as brandy, tobacco, wine, silk and lace were particularly sought after, but no commodity was more cherished (or more valuable) than tea: the English obsession.

The cost of a pound of tea in 1740 was 3d, but with tax added this became 5 shillings, and with 12 pennies to a shilling the potential mark up for contraband tea was considerable. It has since been estimated that 75% of all tea drunk in England around this time had been illegally obtained.

With the excise from imported goods essential to Government coffers, the authorities despaired at the impunity with which smugglers were able to go about their business. But while decent society shook its head in disapproval and expressed horror at the violence the smuggler gangs employed, there was barely a rich man's table that had not been set by the smuggler's hand or a glass uncharged with contraband brandy. Whether it was the smugglers themselves, those who financed their activities, or the people who merely purchased their goods, everyone appeared to benefit except the Government, which remained determined to stamp it out.

With its profits widely dispersed, smuggling had become essential to the prosperity of the coastal economies where it thrived and those whose livelihoods depended upon it were willing to kill in its defence. When Customs Officer Thomas Carswell, accompanied by a troop of dragoons, stumbled across and seized a large shipment of tea hidden in a barn, he hastily set about organising its transportation to a place of safety, but word had spread and James Stanford, a leading member of the Hawkhurst Gang, had already gathered his men and was lying in wait.

Perhaps flush with his success, or merely naive about the possible violence of any response, Carswell took few precautions. As he and his men approached a narrow lane, with little room for manoeuvre, they were greeted by a volley of musket fire that first dispersed the troops before Carswell was singled out, dragged from his horse and shot dead.

Those troops who had not already fled were rounded up, disarmed, stripped, beaten, and forced to walk thirty miles without rest or relief before being released on the promise, on pain of death, never to take up arms again. In the meantime, the Government continued to ratchet up the penalties for smuggling.

In 1718, the Hovering Act made it illegal for vessels under 50 tons to linger offshore and any smaller boats seen sailing to and from such ships were seized. Boats with four or more oars found in the Channel would likewise be intercepted and their crews detained, with those vessels suspected of being used for the transportation of contraband goods sawn in half. This attempt by the Government to stifle the smugglers at source by destroying the tools of their trade was not as effective as might be imagined. Many of the smugglers were fishermen with easy access to other craft and they proved their resourcefulness by simply utilising the sawn-up vessels for other purposes such as storage and even as places of shelter at the location of their criminal endeavours, examples of which can still be seen today.

The smugglers did not consider their trade illegitimate. Although by no means disinclined towards theft for the most part, they paid for their contraband in commercial transactions sealed with a handshake either with the crew of ships, workers in the dockyards, and even on occasions with the Customs officers themselves.

This wasn't always the case of course. The English coastline is perilous and beset with hazards and in unpredictable seas ships would regularly founder. Where there were wrecks there were wreckers: those who flocked to the scene of a shipwreck to take advantage of the opportunities provided by God's wrath. Smuggling communities were always on high alert during storms for cargo washed ashore, which at the time the law determined to be common property. They also kept a close lookout for wrecks close to shore, which would be boarded once the storm had relented to remove the cargo. This wasn't illegal so long as no surviving crew remained aboard. This was as good as a death sentence for any that did. Once the survivors had been killed the ship would be dismantled to hide any trace of the crime.

In foul weather the better-organised smuggler gangs would often light beacons and hang lamps to lure ships on to rocks or sandbanks. 'The lure', as it was known, was a particularly notorious activity in Cornwall, where it was regularly undertaken by ruthless men such as John Carter and Cruel Coppinger.

Customs officers were seen as infringing upon the customary rights of local communities and those who could not be bribed were perceived as dangerous outsiders and met with hostility so intense that it became impossible for them to operate without the protection of armed dragoons. Even then it was unsafe for the customs officers to drink in local taverns or attend county fairs, whether in uniform or not. Customs officers, much like the soldiers who protected him, lived in constant fear of their lives.

In 1736, transportation to the colonies, often as an indentured slave, became the penalty for those who refused to co-operate with customs officials, but such was the level of intimidation that not only did this fail to break the code of silence, but it also became almost impossible to convict suspected smugglers in the local Assizes. People were afraid to come forward and testify against gang members, while the magistrates themselves were often cowed and compliant, simply issuing fines that went unpaid or ordering public whippings that were never carried out.

Indeed, so widespread was smuggling on the south coast that it was arguably an early example of organised crime. The violence was such that it was considered by customs officers to be the most dangerous posting in England. Of all the smugglers operating none were more feared than the Hawkhurst Gang, named after the village in which it was formed in 1735, which came to dominate the area around Kent and Sussex with influence stretching as far west as Dorset and north as far as London and the Thames estuary.

Many people were involved with the Hawkhurst Gang without being actual members: they provided safe houses, acted as lookouts and informers or men for hire, and, with as many as 200 active members, the gang also used the threat of violence to control the areas in which they operated, engaging in deliberate acts of intimidation such as riding in force through villages in broad daylight, stripped to the waist, swords at their side, tattoos resplendent in the gleaming sun.

At the taverns where they met, the Oak and Ivy in Hawkhurst, the Star and Eagle in Gourdestoun, and the Mermaid Inn in Rye, gang members would sit near the entrance, their pistols cocked on the table before them, lookouts posted, and the exits covered while those who passed through the doors were closely monitored. They were also ruthless in the dispensation of what they considered justice.

When a farm labourer, Richard Hawkins, stole two bags of tea from the smuggler Jeremiah Curtis, he was dragged from his home in the dead of night and taken to the Dog and Partridge Inn where he was interrogated and forced into a confession before being clubbed to death and his body thrown down the well of the local landowner Sir Cecil Bishop as a warning to others.

The gang also set out to deliberately humiliate any customs officers unfortunate enough to fall into their hands. At the Old Bailey trial of a smuggler named Poison, customs officer Joseph Boulton described how, after his horse had gone lame and he and his colleagues had taken shelter in a local tavern, they were taken prisoner by the Hawkhurst Gang:

> All of a sudden, we heard a prodigious firing, it was a gang of smugglers – there were eight of them. They came up to the Alehouse and hearing of such a number coming we hid ourselves but they seeing our horses threatened that they would have us and would fire and pull the house down, and upon searching found us and robbed us of our arms and money. They stripped us naked all above the waist and then they began to cut us in the most terrible manner. Then word went up that the Boulogne Boat was coming, and we were put upon horses and tied and taken to the lid-light near the sea. When we came there, I believe there were two hundred horses and a hundred men, some were landing tea in oilskin bags, and I saw a cart pulled by two oxen loaded with port and brandy.

Like the man on trial, Poison, gang members would use aliases such as Diamond, Black Tooth, Yellow Dick and Nasty Jack to shield their identity from the authorities, despite being well known locally.

As Joseph Boulton's testimony shows, the smuggling itself was often carried out on a massive scale, with certain beaches, such as that at Hastings, being flat and low-lying with a grit and shingle surface ideal for hauling boats ashore and making a quick getaway.

In 1744, a shipment of contraband from three ships moored off Pevensey Bay required 200 men to unload it, with dozens of carts and 500 pack horses to carry it all inland. Often the transportation of such large shipments required gangs such as the Groombridge and Mildmay to cooperate and pool their resources, even though they remained bitter enemies. Indeed, on one occasion the Hawkhurst Gang fought and defeated the Wingman Gang in what was little short of a pitched battle.

The places of storage for such huge loads had to be similarly impressive, and one of the most frequently used was the abandoned and derelict Hertsmonceaux Castle near Rye. At night smugglers would wander the ramparts howling, blowing whistles and banging drums to give it the appearance of it being haunted to deter prying eyes. This gave rise to the local legend of the Ghostly Drummer of Hertsmonceaux. Meanwhile, their colleagues secreted the contraband in the tombs that lay in the grounds around it.

Following its temporary storage, when tea would often be adulterated with rose petals to increase its quantity, the larger shipments would be transported at night to London under armed guard where on the outskirts of the city they would be handed over to men who had paid for a delivery or taken to dumps nearby ready for market the following day.

Secrecy remained paramount as palms were greased and deals struck on a nod and a wink, with few words exchanged between the smugglers and the representatives of the rich London merchants who were the main beneficiaries.

Also making the journey to London would be the so-called 'dollop men', who, carrying up to a hundredweight of tea on their person, would make deliveries to specific locations such as shops, taverns and tea and coffee houses. Two such dollop men, George Watson and Jack Hemming, on trial for the murder of an informant, described just such a delivery:

> About seven in the evening, we set out from Redhill, we had three hundred and a quarter of tea. We were in the company of 15 or 16 men and 20 horses. We came through Islington where we separated. Tom Brick and Blue Dick went to a grocer here. We came down Old Street to the Doghouse Tavern and waited with the hundredweight of tea for people who were to fetch from thence. A Watchman came by, he asked, who's there? A friend says I, and I gave him a shilling for drink.

In December 1745, the Jacobite forces of Bonnie Prince Charlie advanced from Scotland as far south as Derby, just 130 miles from London. The city was in a panic and a French invasion in support of his claim to the throne appeared imminent. But it wasn't to be, and Charlie retreated north. When in April 1746 he was decisively defeated at the Battle of Culloden the immediate threat appeared to be over. Even so, the political situation in England remained tense and the close connections between the smugglers of the south coast, where any invasion force could be expected to land, and their French counterparts, added a dangerous political element to what had previously been a merely criminal enterprise.

The suspicion of having Jacobite sympathies was something the Hawkhurst Gang, among others, were willing to exploit if it distracted the authorities from their criminal activities. They were also aware that the fear of a French invasion stretched the Royal Navy to its limits.

So, to meet at a place such as the Oak and Ivy Tavern (oak and ivy were symbols of Jacobite rebellion) was a deliberate provocation, but it was never more than smoke and mirrors. The Government thought otherwise, however, and in 1746 the Act of Indemnity made smuggling a capital offence and, since it was so difficult to secure convictions in the area where the offence occurred, those suspected of it would be tried at the Old Bailey in London.

Only one witness was required to denounce someone as a smuggler, at which point the accused person's name would be published in the *London Gazette* and they would be given forty days in which to hand themselves in. If they did so then a pardon was possible, but if not then a £50 reward would be offered for their capture. Once under lock and key a death sentence would assuredly follow. The Government's attitude was clarified by the then Solicitor-General Sir William Murray, Lord Mansfield, at the trial of a smuggler for murder:

> You need not be told because it is very notorious, the different steps the Government has been forced to take in order, if possible, to get the better of the offence of smuggling. There is no Magistrate or Officer where they reign, if I may say, can put only law in execution against them – it is now a struggle between the Government and this Banditi.

It was an effective declaration of war, but the Government clampdown did little to curtail smuggler activity.

On 22 September 1747, the *Three Brothers,* sailing from Guernsey with 30 hundredweight of contraband tea, numerous sacks of coffee and 70 casks of rum and brandy, was intercepted by the customs vessel *Swift* under the command of Captain William Johnson. It was a haul to the value of £1,000 or more and a great coup for Captain Johnson; delighted with his success he took the contraband to the Customs House at Poole Harbour, where it was placed under armed guard and the protective guns of a warship moored offshore. But word of his success spread quickly.

The crew of the *Three Brothers,* who had escaped the seizure of their ship, rushed to inform Richard Perrin, a leading member of the Hawkhurst Gang and the man who had organised and financed the shipment. He wasn't prepared to let such a valuable cargo slip from his grasp and so agreed to share it with the gang and their associates should they recover it.

On 7 October, some forty smugglers, twelve of whom were Hawkhurst men, arrived in Poole, where they soon realised that any attempt to storm the Customs House would see them come under fire from the warship assigned to protect it. However, those living nearby soon informed them that when the tide ebbed, for a few hours at least, the Customs House would be out of sight to those moored offshore.

In the darkness of early morning, with a sea mist swirling and carrying flaming torches, the smugglers attacked the Customs House. Hearing the fearful noise they made, the guards merely threw open its doors and fled. Anticipating resistance, the smugglers had not expected to recover all the contraband and so had insufficient means by which to take it away and were forced to leave the caskets of and rum and brandy behind. Still, they remained delighted with their haul of tea.

The raid on the Poole Customs House was a direct affront to the Government and worse was to follow when one of the gang members involved, named Diamond, visited a cobbler called Daniel Chater, paying for his services with a small packet of the contraband tea. Not long after this Diamond was arrested. The rumour soon spread that Chater had informed on him for the reward. The rumours appeared to be confirmed when he was called to be a witness at Diamond's subsequent trial.

Accompanied by the Customs Officer William Galley, an elderly gentleman nearing retirement, Chater set off for the village of East

Breaking into the King's Customs House, Poole, Cutters and Smugglers (1700-1855).

Marden, where he was to formally identify Diamond before the local Justice of the Peace.

With neither of the men familiar with the area around East Marden, they soon found themselves lost and spent many hours aimlessly wandering, trying to find their bearings. Exhausted they stopped off at the White Hart Inn near Rowland's Castle, unaware that it was a smugglers' tavern. As they rested and slaked their thirst the landlady, who was aware of their identity, slipped away to inform two of the Hawkhurst Gang, William Carter and William Jackson, of their presence. With some urgency they gathered their men.

Weary from the day's travails, Chater and Galley decided to stay the night. While they slept their clothes were ripped and searched and their purses stolen; then, woken from their slumbers, they were bound, beaten, and tortured over many hours.

The following morning, stripped almost naked, they were tied to horses and taken to the Red Lion Inn at Rake, where their fate would be decided. Having fallen beneath their horses during the ride, their heads bumping and dragging along the ground, the two men were bloodied and barely conscious by the time they arrived.

Galley, who already near death, the smugglers decided to be rid of and so he was taken to a nearby field and buried alive. In the meantime, Chater was chained up in a shed and left without food or water for several days while they deliberated about whether to punish or kill him. Clearly, he was a man who could not be trusted, and the decision was made to kill him. He was taken to Lady Holte Park where he was thrown down a well and had rocks dropped on him until he was dead.

The brutal murder of an elderly Customs Officer and a simple cobbler shocked many people, and the wealthier members of the community now began to fear for both their property and their own lives. In an area where the law no longer appeared to apply, they needed to take matters into their own hands.

In the village of Gouldhurst a militia was formed under the command of George Sturt, a retired soldier, who was determined to wrest control back from the smugglers. This was a direct challenge to the Hawkhurst Gang, in whose territory the village lay, and especially to Thomas Kingsmill, one of its leaders and a native of the village.

The outraged Kingsmill, who had long ruled the roost locally, threatened to loot and burn the village to the ground if the militia was not disbanded and Sturt handed over to the gang. He gave the people until eleven o'clock in the morning on 21 April to comply. When the militia did not disband Kingsmill proved as good as his word, turning up at the appointed time with the Hawkhurst Gang, their numbers bolstered by any number of common thieves and malcontents hoping to share in any booty. But the Gouldhurst militia did not flee, as Kingsmill had expected, and instead took up positions in and around the heavily barricaded church. As the smugglers and their hangers-on approached, many stripped to the waist, waving swords, banging drums, and making a great deal of noise, the militia let loose a volley of musket fire. As the smoke cleared Kingsmill's brother could be seen lying dead along with several others. Following a further exchange of gunfire and some brief hand-to-hand fighting those who had turned up for easy pickings began to flee. The sight of them running for their lives caused others to hesitate. When the cry went up that troops were on the way they too panicked and fled.

The humiliation at Gouldhurst broke the power of the Hawkhurst Gang and ended their reign of terror. Over the next few months many of the leading members, including Thomas Kingsmill, Richard Perrin, William Fairall and Thomas Lillywhite, were arrested, tried at the Old Bailey in London, and hanged. They were just four of the thirty-five smugglers to be executed over the next two years, some of whom were strung up from the fourteen gibbets that dotted the Sussex skyline for the next thirty years.

To resist smuggler violence was not the same as opposition to smuggling itself, however, and the Government's partial success in hunting down and executing some of the leading exponents did little to curtail the practice and local support for it remained strong. As the chaplain of Newgate Prison in London, where many of the smugglers were interned before trial, wrote:

> The common people in general fancy there is nothing in the crime of smuggling. There is no harm done to the community or to public property, they believe it is their right.

Even in 1784, when Prime Minister William Pitt slashed the duty on tea from 129% to just 12.5%, making it unprofitable as contraband, the smugglers merely turned their attentions elsewhere. It wasn't until 1846 and the Repeal of the Corn Laws, when free trade became the economic shibboleth of a rapidly industrialising Britain, that large-scale smuggling ceased to be profitable enough for smugglers to risk the consequences of arrest.

# PART FIVE

# Sex

# Chapter 1

# Virtue and vice

> 'The companion of an evening, and the companion for life, require very different qualifications.'

By the latter half of the eighteenth-century London was the commercial and financial centre of the world, a city of a million souls seething with activity which lay at the heart of a burgeoning empire of trade. It was the place to be seen and to make one's fortune; but it was also Hogarth's London, a cauldron of death and disease, of thievery and hucksterism, a dark place, a

The Orgy, William Hogarth, *The Rake's Progress* Plate 3 (1735) Unknown source. (Public domain via Wikimedia Commons)

threatening, violent and lying place. His was the London of Gin Lane and The Harlot's Progress, a series of paintings and engravings depicting the story of Mary Hackett, soon to be Moll Hackabout, an innocent country girl debauched by drink who sold her body, contracted syphilis and was dead by 24. But if money was London's religion, then sex provided its sin, and if the former was hard to come by the latter was always readily, if seldom freely, available.

Freed from the strictures of religious and political conformity, Georgian Britain was awash with vice. The rigid social conventions and conformity of polite society, both strictly adhered to and, it must be said, honoured as much in the breach, were not reflected lower down the social order. There was little time for such niceties when life was 'nasty, brutish, and short', other than for derision and the age-old tradition of mocking one's betters. Sex was both desired and available and people were as free with their bodies as they were careless of their virtue.

Men seeking sexual gratification outside of the marriage bed was nothing new of course, and the world's oldest profession provided the means for them to do so, with perhaps as many as a third of women in the city selling their bodies at one time or another to make ends meet, and there were at least 20,000 prostitutes plying their trade at any one time.

# Chapter 2

# Prostitutes, their clients, and *Harris's List*

*Harris's List*, published between 1757 and 1795, was a Directory of supposedly respectable prostitutes working in Covent Garden and the streets thereabout.

Widely seen as the pleasure dome of London, Covent Garden was as a beehive to the wealthy young men of the city and those of greater vintage but no less sexual ambition who were looking for a harlot or doxie with whom to spend the night, and its reputation for hedonism spread far and wide. Giacomo Casanova, who knew a thing or two about such things, wrote of Covent Garden that it provided '*a wonderful debauch*'; while James Boswell, the noted biographer of Dr Johnson, was impressed by the variety of entertainment on offer and indeed its value for money: '*from the splendid Madame at 50 guineas a night to the civil nymph who could be had for a pint of wine and a shilling.*'

A Directory of London's prostitutes was not a new phenomenon. After the demise of the Commonwealth demise and the return of dynastic politics in the figure of King Charles II, the 'Merry Monarch', entertainment, the arts and the printed word flourished in a new atmosphere of freedom. In 1660, just months after the King's restoration, *The Wandering Whore* appeared. This publication adopted a conversational tone and followed the experienced bawd Magdalena as she guided the young harlot Julietta through the pitfalls and otherwise of her profession. However, despite declaring itself a warning – beware the exquisite whore and the pimping hector – the hostility of previously puritanical London saw it last only five editions.

Another forerunner of *Harris's List* was '*Kind Women, and Others of the Linen Lifting Tribe*'. Published in 1691, it was less reticent than its predecessor and described in detail those who were for sale: '*Mary Holland is tall, graceful, and comely; shy of her favours but open to persuasion for a fee of around ten pounds.*'

This was indeed expensive and beyond the means of most, and so the magazine went on to say that her sister Elizabeth was indifferent to money and a good supper, and two shillings would suffice.

*Harris's List* took a similar format and tone, providing not just a simple directory of names but also helpful descriptions of the prostitutes themselves: how they looked, their merits, their specialities, and their price.

The *List*, which was quite provocative in its prose, would prove no less pornographic in its use, with a much-thumbed copy greatly sought after by those unable to afford and enjoy the delicacies on offer but desirous of a similarly pleasurable effect.

The charms of Miss Conway of 50 Sloane Square were described thus:

> She has so many enchanting graces, that they are quite irresistible. It is impossible to withstand the artillery of her eyes, as the winged lighting of her hair, her lips, her everything, are so transporting, charming, as to fill every beholder with rapture.

The 1788 entry for Mrs Dodd of 6 Hind Court, Fleet Street adopted a different approach:

> Reared on two pillars of alabaster, the symmetry of its parts, its borders enriched with wavering tendris, its ruby portals, and the tufted grove that crowns the summit of the mount, all join to invite the guest to enter.

The same year Miss Davenport's entry read:

> Her teeth are remarkably fine, she is tall, and so well-proportioned when you examine her full naked figure, which she will permit you to do.

> **Miss Chicamp of 2 York Street:** One of the finest fattest figures, as fully finished for fun and frolic as fertile fortune ever formed.

All sexual persuasions were catered for in Covent Garden and it was said that if a woman seemed unusually tall and wore too much makeup then she was likely a man: not that male prostitutes ever appeared in the

*List*, for sex between men remained the vice that dare not speak its name. This was not so for women: even if the later Victorians would refuse to formally acknowledge the existence of lesbianism, it remained in the public imagination as a higher form of love, and so it was in *Harris's List*:

> **Miss Wilson of Cavendish Square:** As a female bedfellow can give more real joys for a woman than ever, she experienced with the male part of the sex.
>
> **Anne Redshawe:** She will always provide a discreet service for those 'women of the highest keeping.

*Harris's List* would often boast of Covent Garden's high-profile clients, among them the leading Whig politician Charles James Fox, the author Horace Walpole, and even royalty such as Augustus I of Hanover. Indeed, the authors would wax lyrical about such encounters, as for example with this 1764 entry for the supposed visit to Miss Wilmot of King George III's brother Edward, Duke of York:

> He gazed upon her for a while with eyes of transport and fondness, and gave her a world of kisses, at the close of which in a pretended struggle, she contrived matters so artfully that the bedclothes have fallen off her naked beauties lay exposed at full-length. The snowy orbs of her breasts by their frequent rising and falling by beat Cupid's alarm drum to storm instantly in case an immediate surrender should be refused. The coral-lipped mouth of love seemed with kind movements to invite, nay to provoke and attack, while her sighs, and eyes half-closed, denoted that no farther resistance was intended. What followed may be better imagined then described.

The great and the ennobled also frequented the salons and parlours of women who considered themselves courtesans in the French style, who sold more than sex, satisfying the lustful nature of both mind and body. Some would marry their clients: for example, Harriet Powell wed the Earl of Seaforth, while Kitty Fisher, who married Sir John Norris, became a favourite model of the court painter Sir Joshua Reynolds and a celebrity in her own right.

Fetishes were also catered for:

> **The Miss Bryan and Smith Sisters, 7 Windmill Street:** Miss Bryan is tall and thin, her complexion is dark, her sister Miss Smith is plump and fair; the ladies have seen their thirtieth but are still agreeable pieces for the winter season to those not over nice about delicacy both being illiterate and dedicated to swearing; it is said they are both dexterous in the use of the birch and rod; the price of these lecherous girls varies very much, but half a guinea is always acceptable.

Not all entries were complimentary, indicating that some had been shy of paying for a favourable biography:

> **Miss Berry** was almost rotten and her breath cadaverous.
>
> **Miss Jenny Kirkbeard** has a violent attachment to drinking.
>
> **Miss Dean** exhibited great indifference whilst entertaining her client cracking nuts as he acted his joys.

The List also provided insight into the racial and religious diversity of the city.

> **Miss Wilkinson, 27 Litchfield Street:** The land of Jamaica is the native soil of this wanton Cyprian female, though she cannot boast a complexion delicately fair, yet it must be acknowledged her features are very pleasing.
>
> **Miss Lawrie, 6 Church Street:** The religion of the Jews will not permit them to eat pork, or feast with Christians; how strictly this lady may adhere to these particulars in her articles of her faith we cannot positively tell; but this we can say for truth – she has not the least objection to Christian concupiscence and will open her Synagogue of love even on the Sabbath.

The authors of *Harris's List* remained shrouded in secrecy throughout the almost forty years of its existence, for the prying eyes of society's moral guardians, though fewer in number than later generations, were no less outraged. Even in a city where corruption was endemic and infected the highest echelons of the social and political elite there was no immunity from prosecution.

The *List* itself is believed to have originated from John Harrison, a well-known and wealthy Covent Garden pimp who worked from the Shakespeare's Head tavern, where he kept a detailed list of his prostitutes and their clients. These records he shared with the Grub Street hack John Derrick, who used them to produce *Harris's List*. However, the authors remained anonymous to avoid falling victim to the next surge of moral outrage and an inevitable clampdown. But little effort was made to restrict its distribution, and it was openly sold by street vendors and in the taverns and shops in Covent Garden, along the Strand, and in other places where men of means chose to spend their nights. But then *Harris's List* wasn't intended for the common man and few of London's many prostitutes ever appeared in it. Most were 'street harlots', forced to sell their bodies for a penny not a shilling, let alone a pound, merely to eat and often for drink. Men and women copulating was simply what happened and was best

The Covent Garden Morning Frolic, Louis Peter Boitard (1747). British Cartoons Print Collection. (Public domain Wikimedia Commons)

ignored. It was the corruption of wealth and decent society that concerned the powers that be.

In the summer of 1787, following King George III's call for the Encouragement of Piety and Virtue, and the Punishment of Vice, Profuseness, and Immorality, the Proclamation Society was formed. Such a declaration against impropriety had long been sought by those such as William Wilberforce, to add impetus to their campaign to root out sin and moral corruption in high places. Its success in doing so would become evident in the decades to come, but an attempt to likewise improve the morals of the poor would prove more problematic. Yes, sex would become the unspoken vice, but though condemnation dripped readily from the tongues of hypocrites, more pornography was sold and distributed in London during the Victorian era than at any time before that.

One of the first victims of the new moral broom sweeping London clean was *Harris's List,* which, following the arrest, prosecution, and imprisonment of a number of those found to be associated with its production, ceased to be published.

The last edition came out in 1795 following a period of harassment that had seen the quality of writing diminish and its sales decline to three figures from its peak circulation of around 8,000 four years earlier.

# Chapter 3

# The Molly House and Mother Clap

> 'Several were seized in women's apparel. Next day they were carried before the Lord Mayor in the same dress they were taken in. Some were completely rigged in gowns, petticoats, head cloths and laced shoes… some were dressed like milk maids, others like shepherdesses.'

If women so inclined could freely advertise their wares (and I use the term guardedly as it was not entirely absent of injunction) the same could not be said for men whose affections lay elsewhere; and in a city such as London, as much a magnet then as it is today to those who mistakenly believed its streets paved with gold, all sexual proclivities had to be catered for.

Homosexuality, then referred to as sodomy, was not merely thought a vice, but was also a crime punishable by death. Indeed, men were still being hanged for the offence as late as 1835, while homosexuality itself wasn't decriminalised until 1967, but just as you cannot expunge an idea out of existence with the wave of a legislative wand, so it is with same-sex attraction. Homosexuals would gather and they would meet, but they did so in secret, and anonymously.

'Molly' was a term used to describe an effeminate or homosexual man in Georgian times and the Molly Houses named after them were often private rooms put aside in taverns exclusively for men, often dressed as women, to behave accordingly and engage in sex.

Georgian society sought to punish homosexuals for what was thought an unnatural vice and a sin against God. They were no less aware of it than we are today, and the fact that there were Molly Houses was no secret in Georgian England.

Outside the privacy of one's own home, which was in any case rarely private, the Molly House was the only place where a homosexual man, especially an overtly effeminate one, could be himself. It was here, where the emphasis was placed on cross-dressing and gender subversion, that they could indulge their fantasies in a relatively safe environment.

Once in a Molly House men would most often adopt female dress, feminine mannerisms and a female persona. As simply attending a Molly House was enough to put one's life in danger, secrecy was paramount. It was usual for those in attendance to be known only by their female name to others present.

Men Depicting Women, A Transmutation of the Sexes, John Collett (1750). (Public domain via Wikimdia Commons)

Role-play and the mock rituals of femininity played a significant part in the activities and these included sham weddings with the vows administered by a defrocked or fake priest, and with male bridesmaids. A bed would then be provided so the marriage could be consummated.

Along with the subverted re-enactment of traditional courtship it was not unknown for the process of giving birth to be feigned for the amusement of others.

The most notorious such venue was run by Margaret Clap, who owned a coffee shop in Field Street, Holborn, an area of London that was a popular meeting place for homosexuals. Open to the public most days, it was transformed into a Molly House on a Sunday.

It has been estimated there were as many as forty Molly Houses in London at the time, but Mother Clap's was always the most popular. This was because she did not run her establishment merely for profit, but genuinely cared for her clients. She enjoyed their company and even on occasions spoke up in defence of those who had been arrested for reasons of indecency or lewd behaviour. The term 'Mother' was affectionate, reflecting her nurturing and kindly nature. Molly was also an abbreviation of the name Margaret, and though it is not known whether she influenced the use of the term Molly to describe homosexual men, she does seem likely to have been the genesis of the phrase 'to mollycoddle'.

Mother Clap, who always presided over the gatherings at her coffee house in person, and was often known to pop over to the Bunch O' Grapes tavern nearby to purchase beer, wine, and pies for her customers, also provided beds for those who required a little more privacy.

Active in London at the time was the Society for the Reformation of Manners, for whom the proliferation of Molly Houses was a particular concern. They were always looking to bring prosecutions and close establishments down and unknown to Mother Clap her coffee shop had been under surveillance for some time.

However, two former clients of Mother Clap, a jilted and resentful lover, Mark Partridge, and the prostitute and paid informant Thomas Newton, who provided the Society with the information required for the authorities to act, and on 17 February 1726 the Molly House was raided and Margaret Clap, along with forty men, was arrested.

The case against Margaret and her customers relied largely on the testimony of the Bow Street Runner Samuel Stevens, who had attended Mother Clap's on several occasions, posing as Mark Partridge's husband. He testified that:

> Sometimes they sit in one another's laps, kissing in a lewd manner and using their hands indecently. Then they would get up and dance and make curtsies, and mimic the voices of women, "O Fie, Sir! Pray, Sir! Dear, Sir! Lord, how can you serve me so! I swear I'll cry out – you are a wicked devil."

Most of the men arrested were subsequently released without charge, but three were tried, convicted of sodomy, and sentenced to be hanged at Tyburn. They were Thomas Wright, a 32-year-old wool comber; William Griffin, a 43-year-old upholsterer; and Gabriel Lawrence, a 43-year-old milkman. Their occupations are significant because many more prominent men were arrested in Molly Houses but rarely, if ever, shared the same fate.

It was necessary some thought, to make an example of a few to maintain order among the many, because the Molly House was one of the rare places in Georgian England where social barriers came down and it was this as much as the activity involved that was considered a threat to social cohesion.

Margaret Clap was convicted of immoral behaviour, keeping a lewd house, and facilitating sodomy. She was sentenced to two years' imprisonment, but first she was to serve a period in the stocks where, exposed to the elements, deprived of food and water and subject to both verbal and physical abuse, a terrible toll was taken. She never recovered from the experience and died before her sentence was served.

There was little sympathy expressed for those caught *in flagrante delicto* with another of the same sex and no penalty was considered too harsh, including death. As was written at the time: *'Sodomites can expect no pity or compassion, for they commit a crime that is detestable to both God and Man.'*

Mother Clap's Molly House is only recorded as having existed for two years, but this was probably just the period during which it was under investigation. Given its popularity and the notoriety of Margaret Clap herself, the likelihood is that it had been in business for much longer.

# Part Six

# It's a Sin

# Chapter 1

# The *Zong* Incident

On 29 November 1781, becalmed in mid-Atlantic and fearing the spread of disease from overcrowding, Captain Luke Collingwood of the slave ship *Zong* ordered 132 sick black slaves to be thrown overboard.

It was a harsh decision, but a necessary one, he felt, given that the cost of any slaves landed dead or near death from natural causes would be borne by the ship's owners and crew. If they were to be disposed of at sea, however, then the financial liability became the responsibility of the ship's insurers. There was little dissent.

Having resolved the problem for now, Collingwood proceeded to successfully deliver the remainder of his cargo to the slave auction in Jamaica before returning to Liverpool and then to London where the insurance claim was duly made.

Collingwood declared that he had no choice but to dispose of the sick slaves aboard the *Zong* because of water depreciation, but an inventory taken of the ship after docking found that there were a great many barrels of water aboard, more than enough for the journey. The ship's insurers would thus contest the claim.

It had not proved possible to keep the shocking events aboard the *Zong* a secret, and when they were brought to the attention of the anti-slavery campaigner Granville Sharp he tried to bring a private prosecution against the ship's owners for murder.

This was not the first time Sharp had become involved in an anti-slavery court case; ten years earlier he had helped achieve a landmark ruling when a reluctant Attorney-General Lord Mansfield, after considerable prevarication, had to concede that an American slave, James Somersett, who had since been captured and imprisoned by his master to await transportation back to America after 56 days on the run in London, was being illegally held and should be released on the grounds that slavery did not exist in Britain. The ruling applied only to the specific case under review and not generally, but it was significant nonetheless and was to provide the reference point in all such future cases.

The Somersett decision had been a personal triumph for Sharp, but he would be less successful with the *Zong* prosecution, with the recently appointed Attorney-General Sir John Lee dismissing the case out of hand:

> What is this claim that human people were thrown overboard. This is a case of chattels and goods. Blacks are goods and properties. It is madness to accuse well-serving and honourable people of murder. The case is the same as if wood had been thrown overboard.

Granville Sharp may have failed to bring a criminal prosecution against the ship's owners for murder, but the publicity generated caused shock and outrage, providing momentum to a campaign that had in recent times often appeared moribund.

But while the morality of the slave trade could be questioned, its profitability could not. Indeed, in the eighteenth century there were few trades as lucrative as the one in slaves, with port cities in England such as Bristol and Liverpool being transformed by the income generated from it. There is also no doubt that the economy of the country benefitted from the trade in human lives, with the industrial revolution then already underway in part at least financed by it. Moreover, with the harvesting of cotton in the American south and the cutting of sugar cane on the plantations of the Caribbean so labour intensive, it seemed a trade with a bright future – there could never be too many slaves.

This is not to single out Britain for its involvement in the slave trade, for slavery was commonplace the world over in all cultures and all societies. Very few Britons ever owned a slave, and they were never used to work down the mines or toil long hours in the fields or factories. In that respect Britain has never been a slave-owning society, but it was increasingly utilitarian, and business was business. Some even justified it as a moral good with the paternal aspects of slavery seen as necessary for the civilising of the savage races.

The first slave ship had sailed from Bristol for the African Continent in 1697, one of 2,108 that were to do so before 1807, carrying around 300,000 black men, women, and children into captivity on the sugar and cotton plantations of the Caribbean and the Americas, making Bristol for a time the wealthiest city outside of London.

By 1740, however, Bristol's pre-eminence in human trafficking had been surpassed by Liverpool, which though coming late to the slave trade had a greater capacity, which saw it expand rapidly. In 1792, for example, 131 slave ships sailed from Liverpool, 42 from Bristol, and 22 from London. By 1795, Liverpool controlled 80 per cent of the British and 40 per cent of the European slave trade. Despite this, however, it never represented more than 10 per cent of Liverpool's overall trade and so, unlike in Bristol, it did not contribute significantly to the city's greater prosperity, though it made many merchants very rich.

Many smaller ports also prospered from the slave trade, as did the many businesses that provided it with goods and services and those who invested in it. Any campaign to restrict or abolish slavery would then have to overcome a powerful lobby and a vested interest that lay at the very heart of commerce in Britain.

The campaign against the slave trade, led for the most part, though not exclusively, by the non-conformist religions such as the Quakers and the Methodists, was rarely lacking in commitment and passion, but often lacked cohesion, any sense of strategy, and, more importantly, influence.

John Wesley, one of the co-founders of Methodism, had long campaigned against the iniquities of slavery, but though his voice was often heard it was rarely listened to. In 1788, now an old man and in ill-health, he journeyed to Bristol to preach against slavery one last time, and though his body was weak his ardour remained as he made an impassioned plea for justice and humanity:

> Give liberty to whom liberty is due, that is, to every child of man, to every partaker of human nature. Let none serve you, but by his own act and deed, by his own voluntary action. Away with all whips, all chains, all compulsion. Be gentle to all men; and see that you invariably do with everyone as you would he should do unto you.

Wesley's messages were not always well received, and the windows of the chapel were installed in its roof to prevent them being smashed, and the pulpit raised high and blocked off from the congregation to protect the speaker.

The *Zong* affair had not only provided the anti-slavery campaign with renewed vigour, but also new leadership. No longer would the burden of supporting abolition fall repeatedly upon the careworn if venerable shoulders of the elderly John Wesley and the cloistered and otherworldly Granville Sharp. Now the much younger Thomas Clarkson, son of an Anglican clergyman, became committed to abolishing slavery while at university.

In 1785 he researched what would become a prize-winning essay on the subject and he would later remark that completing it had been like a revelation from God: '*A thought came into my mind, that if the contents of the essay be true it was time* for *some person to bring their calamities to an end.'* He would dedicate the rest of his life to ending not just the trade in slaves, but slavery itself.

It was Clarkson's essay that brought him to the attention of Sharp and others, and it soon became clear just how much they needed him. With boundless energy he toured the country visiting all the major ports, speaking to the sailors who worked aboard the ships, and purchasing the tools of the trade – the manacles, and instruments of punishment and torture – to display to the public the cruelty and wickedness of slavery.

Clarkson addressed audiences in the very places where he was least welcome: in the taverns overlooking the harbours where the ships were moored waiting to depart for Africa, and the meeting houses where the deals were struck, contracts signed, and money exchanged. Often subject to great hostility, he would remove from his bag and hold up for all to see the chains of human bondage, and he wasn't afraid to remind his audience of the source of their great wealth: their splendid homes, their delicate silks, their fine wines, and their gracious living.

Attempts were made on Clarkson's life, but the very fact that people were willing to kill for the right to enslave others was proof of slavery's corruption of the human spirit. It only served to embolden him further.

In May 1787, the 'Committee for the Abolition of the Slave Trade' was formed, with Clarkson, Granville Sharp, the businessman Josiah Wedgwood and the playwright Hannah More among its more prominent members.

That same year Wedgwood, who had made his money in ceramics, produced his famous medallion with the image of a slave in chains and the words – '*Am I not a man and a brother'*. This would become the mantra of the campaign.

As the title of the Committee indicates, its members were not campaigning to abolish slavery as such. This, they believed, was beyond their means, entailing as it would the deprivation of property, claims for compensation, and years of endless litigation. And that was if they were successful, which they doubted they would be. The detrimental economic impact of slavery's abolition guaranteed it would be fought for tooth and nail by the plantation owners of the Indies who were dependent upon black labour for their profits. It seemed better to focus on ending the trade in slaves. Not all agreed but it was at least a first step.

Am I Not a Man and a Brother, Josiah Wedgwood (1789). (Official Medallion of the British Anti-Slavery Society)

The formation of the Committee provided the anti-slavery movement with the cohesion it had previously lacked, but it remained outside the decision-making process. It required a representative in Parliament, someone of influence and gravitas who could carry the campaign into the corridors of power – but who could they approach?

William Wilberforce was born in Hull on 24 August 1759, the only son of a wealthy merchant who, unlike so many others in the city, made his money trading goods not people.

When he was nine, his father died and his mother, struggling to cope with the loss of her husband, sent the young William to live with his relatives in London. There he remained for three years before his mother, concerned that he might be absorbing his uncle's non-conformist religious views, brought him back to Hull. It made little difference for he was to prove non-conformist by nature.

In 1783, Wilberforce attended St John's College, Cambridge where he was a contemporary of the future Prime Minister William Pitt at nearby Pembroke, who would become one of his closest friends.

Pitt was to prove a constant source of encouragement to his friend throughout his campaign to abolish the slave trade, particularly during those dark moments of despair, of which there were many; but either unwilling or unable to do so he did little to facilitate its progress through Parliament during his tenure as Prime Minister, much to Wilberforce's frustration and very great disappointment.

William Wilberforce, John Russell. (Public domain via WikiArt)

A sociable and independently wealthy man (the result of several inheritances), the young Wilberforce embraced the good life: drinking, gambling and attending the theatre. Despite being physically unimpressive, with the pallor of ill-health that made him appear sick even when he wasn't, his charm and erudition saw him favourably considered by the ladies. He was in those early days far removed from the stern, puritanical figure we recognise today. But he was also a young man who had a very high opinion of himself and believed he was destined for great things – he just didn't know what.

In September 1780, aged twenty-one, Wilberforce became the Member of Parliament for his home town of Kingston-Upon-Hull with the intention of making his mark and doing good. However, the frustrations of parliamentary politics soon bore down upon him and he found that the private member's bills he presented for the moral improvement of the people were either rejected at their second reading in the House of Commons or dismissed out of hand once they were introduced in the House of Lords.

Disappointed, William took solace as he always did at the card tables of the gentlemen's clubs he frequented, and in the bawdier entertainments of late-night London. But his frustration remained.

In October 1784, he embarked upon a Grand Tour of Europe, a rite of passage for any young man or woman of means, returning a year later having undergone some sort of religious conversion. He now doubted whether the combative arena of politics was a suitable place for a man of God and considered resigning as an MP on the grounds of conscience. He was dissuaded from doing so by his friend Pitt and John Newton, the ex-slaver turned clergyman, and author of the hymn *Amazing Grace*. He could do God's work better from inside Parliament, they told him, than he ever could from without. He agreed and so would continue to serve God not in the cloistered world of solitude, prayer, and quiet contemplation, but in the sphere of public life.

Wilberforce's reputation as an independent, refusing to ally with either Whig or Tory, his conversion to Christian Evangelism and his subsequent joining of the Clapham Sect, a group of Christian social reformers and activists, soon came to the attention of those campaigning to end the moral outrage that was the slave trade.

It was Charles Middleton, a naval captain who was himself an MP, but one with poor debating skills, who suggested that the independently-minded Wilberforce might be persuaded to take up the cudgel for the anti-slavery cause in Parliament. It was agreed that Thomas Clarkson should contact Wilberforce, and he visited him at his home in Old Palace Yard, Westminster, within sight of the House of Commons, armed with his essay and his box of slavery paraphernalia. He then proceeded to explain in detail the appalling conditions aboard slave ships and the harsh treatment of the slaves themselves.

Wilberforce listened intently as Clarkson described how on any slave ship the men taken below would be chained to their bunks, unable to stand up or move about, and forced to urinate and defecate where they lay. How the air was so putrid, and the smell so foul, that disease was commonplace and widespread. It was little better for the women and children quartered on deck, exposed to the elements and vulnerable to sexual assault and rape. The slaves were also subjected to beatings, torture, and the humiliation of having to dance for and entertain their captors.

So awful was the journey from Africa to the Americas, the so-called Middle Passage, that it has been estimated that tens of thousands of slaves died before ever reaching their destination. To illustrate the deprivations endured by these 'poor unfortunate wretches' Clarkson would later produce his famous layout of the slave ship *Brookes*.

Little of this was unknown to Wilberforce, who had discussed such things before, but Clarkson, with his power of persuasion and the facts to hand, could convey the reality better than most. The two men spoke for some time, but Clarkson made no proposal other than to suggest they should meet again.

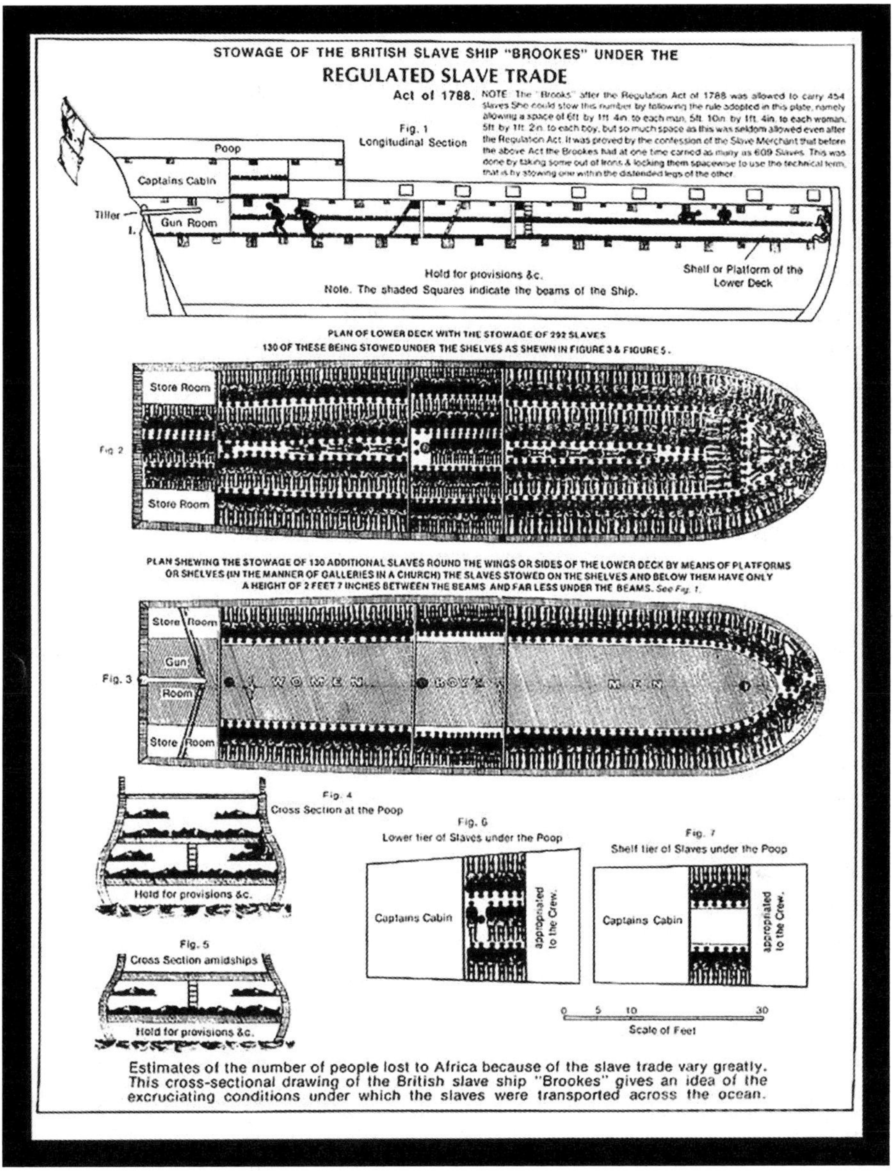


Estimates of the number of people lost to Africa because of the slave trade vary greatly. This cross-sectional drawing of the British slave ship "Brookes" gives an idea of the excruciating conditions under which the slaves were transported across the ocean.

Layout of the slave ship ***Brookes*** as shown to the parliamentary committee investigating the slave trade. (Public domain via Wikimedia Commons)

On 13 March 1787, Wilberforce was invited to a dinner party at the home of Bennet Langton, a committed abolitionist like many of the other guests, among them the artist Sir Joshua Reynolds, and James Boswell, the biographer of Samuel Johnson.

The conversation, though it ranged over many things, kept returning to the subject of injustice – how could there ever be social reform or an improved morality when the original sin of slavery stalked the streets of the nation and haunted the corridors of power, when the profits from slavery constructed municipal buildings, and the blood of slaves signed the documents of every commercial transaction?

At the end of what had been a convivial if at times passionate evening of discussion and debate, the request was put to Wilberforce that he be the anti-slavery campaign's representative in Parliament. The details of the role were left vague and though he listened with interest he remained non-committal, as he was under no illusions about the magnitude of the task. He would, he knew, be opposed not just by the commercial vested interests, the financial institutions, and a landed aristocracy that had in large part seen its fortunes restored by investments in a trade they would often shrug their shoulders at as if in complete ignorance, but also large majorities in both Houses of Parliament against any change in the status quo.

On 12 May, a still undecided Wilberforce was sitting beneath the large oak tree that dominated the grounds of his estate at Holwood, discussing the request made to him by the Anti-Slavery Committee with his friend Pitt and another future prime minister, Lord Grenville, when Pitt interjected:

> William, why don't you give notice of a motion on the subject of the Slave Trade? You have already taken great pains to collect the evidence and so are entitled to the credit that will come to you. Do not lose time, or the ground will be occupied by another.

Wilberforce prevaricated for a time but soon his mind was made up. He had at last found the cause he had been looking for.

On 22 May, the first meeting of the Society for Effecting the Abolition of the Slave Trade took place, delighted to have Wilberforce to campaign for them. But they were disappointed that he declined to join the Society itself or serve on its committee. Even so, Wilberforce firmly believed he had found a cause worth fighting for. He wrote:

> My first years in Parliament I did nothing, nothing to any purpose, my own distinction being my darling object.

His campaign, however, would be delayed by ill-health, possibly the result of a nervous reaction to the burden he now knew he had to bear. In the meantime, the anti-slavery campaign was given a boost with the publication of Olaudah Equiano's biography.

Olaudah Equiano, who preferred to be known by his given name of Gustavus Vassa, had either been taken from Africa as a child or had been born into slavery in colonial South Carolina. His own account and the evidence appear to conflict.

Having briefly laboured on the plantations he spent most of his time at sea, during which he was sold several times. His last master was Robert King, a Quaker who, perhaps feeling pangs of guilt at owning a slave at all, permitted Equiano to earn the money with which he could in time purchase his own freedom, which he did in 1766, aged twenty-one.

Equiano was to remain at sea for some time before finally settling in London where he felt safe from possible kidnap and an enforced return to slavery. In London he joined a group of fellow black men, freed and escaped slaves, called the Sons of Africa, formed to campaign against the slave trade. The fact there were black abolitionists in the commercial centre of the slave trade was possible because of the number of black grooms and valets in England and the thriving, if small, black communities in London and the other major port cities.

It was Equiano who had first brought the case of the *Zong* to Granville Sharp's attention, and it was his description of his life as a slave and its torments that caused a sensation and sold many copies, running through six editions in a very short time.

In the absence of Wilberforce from Parliament, William Pitt acted on his behalf, introducing the motion for a bill on the abolition of the slave trade before, concerned that he would lose support within the House of Commons were he seen as partisan, withdrawing from the issue.

On 12 May 1789, his health restored, William Wilberforce stood up in the House of Commons to make his first great speech against the slave trade. He spoke of its iniquities, with sadness at the absence of justice, but based his arguments for its abolition not on a sense of moral outrage, but on the evidence, compiled over many years from various reports, inquiries held, and verbatim accounts from those involved. He apportioned no blame, he said, but instead appealed to the common humanity and decency in all:

> I wish exceedingly, in the outset, to guard both myself and the House from entering into the subject with any sort of passion.

> It is not their passions I shall appeal to—I ask only for their cool and impartial reason; and I wish not to take them by surprise, but to deliberate, point by point, upon every part of this question. I mean not to accuse anyone, but to take the shame upon myself, in common, indeed, with the whole parliament of Great Britain, for having suffered this horrid trade to be carried on under their authority. We are all guilty—we ought all to plead guilty, and not to exculpate ourselves by throwing the blame on others; and I therefore deprecate every kind of reflection against the various descriptions of people who are more immediately involved in this wretched business.

Wilberforce would detail the cruel reality of taking people forcibly from their homes, of the pain of separation, and the hardships of the voyage; of the cramped conditions, the filth and disease, and the arbitrary use of punishment to maintain control. He exposed the lies that were peddled to mask these truths to spare the feelings of those concerned, to hide the facts that could only prick the conscience of any man. He then beseeched his fellow Members of Parliament to vote in favour of abolishing this 'trade founded in iniquity.'

The speech concluded to a lukewarm reception, followed by the suggestion that before any vote be taken on the motion, the evidence he had produced should be properly scrutinised in committee. Wilberforce agreed: a decision that was later criticised for having seriously impeded the anti-slavery campaign at a time when it appeared to have momentum.

Wilberforce's opponents in Parliament, led by the hero of the American Revolutionary War and MP for Liverpool Banastre Tarleton, were delighted, but if they thought his decision to go to committee had effectively mothballed the campaign they were sorely mistaken, for he was to prove a determined and relentless adversary. Likewise, the pro-slavery lobby in Parliament would fight an aggressive and protracted defence of the institution.

The moral case for the abolition of the slave trade had been made, but its opponents had the Blue Books, the economic facts laying out the harm abolition would do to commerce, the letters and depositions of the plantation owners predicting economic ruin were any restrictions at all placed on the safe and regular delivery of robust slaves to replenish their always depreciating stock of labour. But they too were willing to argue the moral case. It was clear was it not, that:

1. Slavery which has existed since antiquity is common to man.
2. Servitude is the natural condition of the black race.
3. With slavery comes the benefits of Christianity or how the black races would eventually be freed from barbarism and able to participate as free men in civilised society.
4. It was a pleasure to be in the service of a kind master and to be provided with all things.

In July 1789, revolution erupted in France and foreign affairs would dominate Parliamentary debate for months and years to come. Even so, on 18 April 1791, Wilberforce once again introduced his bill in the House of Commons, this time with an impassioned plea:

> Never, never will we desist till we have wiped away this scandal from the Christian name, released ourselves from the load of guilt, under which we at present labour, and extinguished every trace of this bloody traffic, of which our posterity, looking back to the history of these enlightened times, will scarce believe that it has been suffered to exist so long a disgrace and dishonour to this country.

Regardless of the passion and the well-chosen words, when the vote was taken the bill was rejected by 163 to 88, a scale of defeat that surprised Wilberforce. Undeterred, the following year he tried again. This time, however, the Government hijacked the process and proposed a compromise solution, which would address both the concerns of the slave owners and lead to the slave trade's eventual abolition. The motion was easily carried by 230 votes to 85, but Wilberforce was no fool and for eventual he read never.

The Government's attempt to sideline the issue caused a great deal of resentment, with Wilberforce particularly upset, for there was little doubt that he had been sold out by Pitt and others he might once have considered friends. Yet he remained undaunted and in February 1794 he returned once more to Parliament and this time his bill to abolish the slave trade was defeated by just eight votes. It appeared that the anti-slavery campaign had regained some momentum, but this was about to change.

In April 1794, now revolutionary and republican France declared war on Britain. It was to prove a protracted and a ruinously expensive conflict that was to see any proposal which interfered with British trade as an unpatriotic act and those who advocated for it as dangerous radicals.

The opponents of abolition in the House of Commons saw this as their opportunity and all decorum was brushed aside as, orchestrated by Tarleton, they jeered at and heckled those who spoke in favour of abolition, accusing them of being Radicals and Jacobins, which appeared confirmed when the National Convention in France abolished slavery and Wilberforce foolishly suggested to Pitt that he seek a peace settlement. Now every time an MP rose in the House to speak against slavery they were accused of treason and shouted down. Soon they began to absent themselves from its proceedings. When Pitt ordered the arrest of those who had long been campaigning for parliamentary reform on charges of sedition the message was clear.

By the summer of 1795, a disappointed and exhausted Wilberforce was convalescing at home, Thomas Clarkson, suffering from ill-health, had retired to the Lake District, and the Committee for Effecting the Abolition of the Slave Trade had ceased to meet. Many others had been intimidated into silence.

The campaign to end the trade in human lives appeared to be moribund, but Wilberforce persisted nonetheless, introducing his Bill in Parliament time and again. Its adherents remained no less committed, and in 1804 the campaign received a boost when Napoleon Bonaparte reintroduced slavery in the French colonies, turning the campaign to abolish it in Britain from a treasonable act into a patriotic one.

# Chapter 2

# Abolition

On 23 January 1806, William Pitt died aged just 46, an event which, despite some estrangement between the two men, greatly upset Wilberforce. However, although it may not have seemed so at the time, Pitt's passing would prove a blessing in disguise, as the new prime minister, Lord Grenville, was more sympathetic to the anti-slavery cause, and pro-actively so. He decided to introduce the Anti-Slave Trade Bill in the House of Lords, thereby overcoming its greatest obstacle first, so that when it was then sent to the House of Commons it would be almost as a *fait accompli.*

When, on 23 February 1807, the Anti-Slave Trade Bill came before the House of Commons, it was Government sponsored and introduced not by Wilberforce but by the Foreign Secretary Charles Grey. After ten hours of debate, during which Banastre Tarleton appeared to be almost a lone voice in opposition, it was passed by an overwhelming 283 votes to 16. Wilberforce, who was present, wept as his supporters crowded around to congratulate him.

Some now wanted him to push on and demand the abolition of slavery in its entirety, but, overcome with emotion, weary, and not wanting to jeopardise what had already been achieved, he declined to do so.

The Slave Trade Act received Royal Assent on 25 March 1807 and came into effect on 1 May. The last slave ship to leave British shores was the *Amelia Kitty,* which sailed on 27 July. It was able to do so because the contract had been signed before the law was passed (and the British have always been slaves to the law).

Britain's commitment to ending the slave trade was absolute, however, and the law was rigorously enforced. Between 1808 and 1860, at the cost of more than 2,000 sailors' lives, the Royal Navy's West Africa Squadron bombarded and destroyed slaver strongholds, arrested and executed slave traders, and intercepted some 1,600 slave ships and freed between 150,000 and 200,000 slaves.

After twenty years of endless campaigning, broken promises and betrayals, vile mudslinging and public mockery, the evil of the slave trade had been eradicated from British commercial life. It would be far from Wilberforce's only achievement, but it would always be his finest.

Despite his relationship with William Pitt having soured, Wilberforce remained loyal to his old friend, speaking in favour of and supporting him in Parliament even if it meant voting for repressive wartime measures. Indeed, his politics often appeared not to mirror his commitment to social reform. Besides his opposition to the slave trade, he also campaigned against vice and immorality, for animal welfare, for legislation to restrict the use of child labour, and penal reform, while at the same time voting in favour of press censorship, the criminalising of trade unions and against Catholic Emancipation and an Inquiry into the Peterloo Massacre.

In 1821 Wilberforce handed over the reins of the anti-slavery campaign in Parliament to Thomas Fowell Buxton, but he remained its figurehead, writing often in support of slavery's abolition and from time to time once again taking up the cudgel of debate.

The last decade of Wilberforce's life was blighted by ill-health and failing eyesight and though the argument against slavery had long since been won, it appeared that he would not live long enough to see its formal abolition.

The 1832 Reform Act, of which he approved with reservations, extended the franchise to many of the towns and cities of the industrialised north, where abolitionist sentiment was at its strongest, and many of their elected representatives to Parliament shared that sentiment. So when, in May 1833, the Whig Government introduced the Abolition of Slavery Bill, it met little formal opposition.

On 26 July Wilberforce, convalescing at home, was visited by friends who informed him that the abolition of the slave trade throughout the British Empire was certain. Three days later, aged seventy-three, he died and was buried in Westminster Abbey not far from his friend William Pitt.

The Abolition of the Slave Trade Act was passed into law the following month on 28 August 1833.

# Chapter 3

# A Black Man's Experience in Britain

Racism did not exist as a concept in Georgian Britain, but there was certainly prejudice. Difference breeds it, and someone of colour would have been subject to the same prejudice as Jews, Irish, Catholics and foreigners in general, but it was possible for such people to prosper in a country where, prejudice aside, there were few restrictions applied to prevent them from doing so. One such man was Tom Molyneaux.

Tom was a bare-knuckle boxer from Virginia who, having been born into slavery, had been granted his freedom for winning his owner a great deal of money in a prize fight. He immediately moved north to New York, but, still feeling unsafe, he soon took ship for England where he could escape the fear of ever being returned to slavery.

Settling in London, Tom teamed up with another black man, Bill Richmond, who was a successful boxing trainer and owed his own gym. It would prove a fruitful partnership and lead to one of the most famous sporting events of the entire Georgian era.

With his reputation as a pugilist already established, and having impressed in the gym, the purse was put up for Molyneaux to fight for the heavyweight title against the great English hero, Tom Cribb.

Molyneaux was sceptical at first: no such offer would ever be made in the country of his birth, where it would be another 100 years before a black man was able to fight for the title. Once assured of its veracity, however, he leapt at the opportunity.

The two men met at Shenington Hollow in Oxfordshire on 3 December 1810, with Molyneaux very much the outsider. Cribb was thought to be the best pound-for-pound fighter in the world and the contest wasn't expected to last long, but Molyneaux proved to be surprisingly adept, deceptive of movement, quick on his feet, and fast with his fists, leaving an increasingly befuddled Cribb holding on for dear life. With the bout continuing until one of the boxers was either knocked out or quit, things were looking grim for Cribb, who in his desperate attempts to avoid the rain of blows had turned the fight into a wrestling match.

Squaring Up, Cribb versus Molyneaux, George Cruickshank (1811). (Public domain via Wikimedia Commons)

An already restless crowd were becoming increasingly disgruntled at the spectacle and the prospect of their hero losing. As the referee tried to part the fighters Cribb collapsed to the canvas and, according to the rules, now had 30 seconds in which to recover his senses and return to the centre of the ring where a line had been scratched (hence the term coming up to scratch). Meanwhile, elements of the crowd had invaded the ring and in the ensuing chaos the referee lost not only control of the situation, but also of the count. Cribb did eventually return to the centre of the ring, but well outside the time permitted to do so. Meanwhile, and unknown to those watching, in the mêlée Molyneaux had broken his hand. In great pain, and unable to use his right hand, he wanted to quit, but Richmond knew that if he did so they would lose their share of the purse. Forced to continue, the fight now turned decisively in Cribb's favour and, landing a crushing blow on the defenceless Molyneaux's jaw, he ended it in the thirty-fifth round.

Cribb may have retained his title, but to those watching and the many journalists who now wrote glowingly of his abilities, it was clear that the ex-slave Tom Molyneaux had been cheated.

Upon their return to London, both Molyneaux and Richmond were greeted by streets lined with cheering crowds and standing ovations whenever they entered a room. People wanted to shake the boxer by the hand, journalists sought his life story, artists wanted to paint his portrait. He had become, to all intents and purposes, Britain's first black celebrity.

This remained the case even when Molyneaux lost the subsequent rematch, again by knock out. He had not cut the fine figure of a man he had in the first fight, and it was rumoured that he had been enjoying his fame a little too much.

Having lost to Cribb for a second time, Molyneaux split from Richmond and embarked upon a tour of Britain, where despite often beating the local favourite he remained popular, drawing great crowds and making a lot of money. Alas, he squandered the money gambling almost more quickly than he could earn it. Sometimes the reception he received was almost too warm and heavy drinking was taking its toll. Not long after journeying to Ireland for a series of exhibition bouts, he was found dead, possibly of a heart attack. He was just thirty-four years of age.

## Part Seven

# Riot, Treason, Rebellion, and Conspiracy

The Gordon Riots, Charles Green. (Public domain via Wikimedia Commons)

At variance with popular belief often lies the truth, and one such belief that must be taken with a generous pinch of salt is that Britain has a proud tradition of religious toleration. It may have been less severe in its punishments than many of its European neighbours, but it was no more accepting of religious dissent for that. In Britain's case it was for the most part anti-Catholicism. In Georgian Britain, those who professed the Catholic faith might no longer be subject to the threat of torture and death, but they were still unable to worship freely, graduate from university, accept a commission in the army, work for the civil service, or be elected to parliament, among other things. Many of these prohibitions also applied to non-conformists such as Quakers and Unitarians.

Georgian Britain was a tinderbox, easy to ignite and 'collective bargaining by riot' was already commonplace. It didn't take much to rouse the people to violence, as in 1768, when seven people were shot dead by troops at Lambeth in London during protests in defence of the radical MP John Wilkes, who had been jailed for libelling the king. But this was by no means the worst such incidence.

# Chapter 1

# No Popery!

In 1778, the Whig politician Sir George Savile moved in Parliament his Bill intended to remove some of the penalties imposed upon Catholics still outstanding from previous legislation. For the most part any reforms were insignificant, except for the one that would see Catholics who wished to join the army exempt from the requirement to take an oath that was little short of a renunciation of their faith.

Britain was, at the time, trying to suppress its rebellious American subjects who, along with their allies in France, Spain, and the Dutch Republic, were threatening to turn a local conflict into a global war. As a result, the nation's resources were overstretched, and it was hoped that Sir George's planned legislation would provide a much-needed boost to recruitment; for this reason alone, it was supported by Lord North and passed into law as the Catholic Relief Act.

The passage of the Bill was expected to be controversial, it being so easy to stir up anti-Catholic sentiment in England, but any opposition to it was anticipated to be brief and little more than the usual hot air. After all, the Jacobite menace had long since been laid to rest and Catholicism in general no longer posed a threat in staunchly Protestant England.

Even so, for an administration as deeply unpopular as Lord North's, and one so regularly criticised and lampooned in the press for its mishandling of the American Affair, it presented an element of risk.

Sir George had little care for Lord North's priorities, and in passing the Bill he was seeking to ease the restrictions placed upon Catholics that prevented them from fully participating in the life of the nation. For many this was a step too far and set a dangerous precedent which, if repeated, would see Rome once again with its hands on the throat of English liberty, for all knew what Catholicism meant: a return to absolutism, the Inquisition, superstition, and *auto da fe* in the streets of English towns and cities. It could not and would not be tolerated and the new legislation would see the revival of the Protestant Association under the leadership of its charismatic if somewhat eccentric new President, Lord George Gordon. He had already fought successfully to prevent the Catholic Relief Act becoming law in mostly Calvinist Scotland, and now he would seek to do so in England, by bringing his campaign south to London and to the doors of Parliament itself.

Although he was born in London and educated at Eton, Lord George was a Scots nobleman of the Gordon Clan who, as a third son and unlikely to inherit, chose the Royal Navy for his career. He had already enlisted by the age of twelve.

Promoted to the rank of lieutenant, he was never popular with his fellow officers who thought him not only a little odd but too close to the men to be fully trusted. When, in 1773, the First Lord of the Admiralty, the Earl of Sandwich, refused him command of his own ship, he resigned his commission having received several endorsements that suggested a political career beckoned: he was right.

In the General Election of 1774, George was returned as the Member of Parliament for the Constituency of Ludgershall, one of the notorious Pocket Boroughs that were available either for purchase or in the gift of the local landowner or peer.

To suggest that Lord George was a maverick would be to understate the case: temperamental and outspoken, he was highly critical of the Prime Minister Lord North, but no less so of his great rival the Radical leader Charles James Fox. Critical of all and supportive of none made him beloved of no one, a situation little improved by his vocal support for the American colonists in their struggle against the British Crown. But now he had found a cause closer to home.

Popular with the people, whom he was never shy of addressing, as much for his colourful use of the vernacular and unusual demeanour as he was for his views, the authorities, always wary of the next charlatan or demagogue, attempted to placate Sir George and he was to have several private meetings with the king. These continued until George III could bear it no longer and (with some irony given future events) declared Lord George completely mad and banned him from the Royal Court.

London by the 1780s was already a teeming metropolis, the commercial and financial centre of the world, a place of grandeur and display where a man could make his mark and his fortune; but with over a million inhabitants, and increasing daily, its dark alleys and narrow streets were overcrowded, filthy, and rife with disease. Drunkenness and licentious behaviour were commonplace and with a thriving criminal underworld of violence and disorder ever simmered beneath the surface.

With little law and order to speak of (there were of course magistrates, watchmen, and the recently instituted Bow Street Runners to make arrests, but no police presence on the streets) London was a place of riot waiting to happen. It was never a case of 'if' but 'when': it was a city on a knife edge.

The dread of the mob in London was acutely felt and not dissimilar to that expressed by the elite of Rome a thousand years before. There was a genuine fear that a demagogic figure would rouse the people to such a pitch of fury and hatred that the violence and destruction would be so intense as to be uncontrollable and would turn its rage not upon property, but the institutions of state. Had that figure arrived in the person of Lord George Gordon? It seemed so to some, but not to others.

The Protestant Association had been propagandising for some months, with the sermons of popular preachers such as Rowland Hill and Erasmus Middleton well attended and influential. The ground had been well laid, and Lord George now exhorted the people to follow him on a march on the centre of power and he demanded they come in their tens of thousands. If not, then he wouldn't march at all, and the Jesuits could return with their rosary beads and the rack.

Having assembled at St George's Fields in Southwark on 2 June 1780, with Lord George at their head, some 50,000 people, described as 'the better kind of tradesperson', set off in procession for the Houses of Parliament in Westminster, intending to lend their support to Lord George as he delivered in person their petition demanding the immediate repeal of the Catholic Relief Act and an assurance from the Government that there would be no further moves towards Catholic Emancipation.

Many of the marchers wore the blue cockade of the Protestant Association in their hats while others carried flags and banners emblazoned with the words 'No Popery' and suchlike. The mood was boisterous rather than violent, but this would change as tens of thousands of ordinary Londoners swelled the ranks and soon it would not be flags being waved but effigies being burned that dominated the London skyline. By the time the marchers neared their destination the column stretched back four miles.

A local storekeeper, Ignatius Sancho, left us a description:

> At least 100,000 were miserable, ragged rabble from 12 to 60 years of age, besides half as many women and children all parading in the streets, the park, on the bridge, ready for any and every mischief.

The Parliament building was largely undefended but for a few elderly doormen and some of the younger MPs who were up for a fight, but they had little choice but to allow Lord George to deliver his petition:

> Lord George came into the House of Commons with an unembarrassed countenance and a blue cockade in his hat, but finding it gave offence he took it and put it in his pocket, but not before a Captain Herbert, one of the Members threatened to pull it out, while Colonel Murray, another Member warned him that should the mob break into the House he would be the first victim.

But the crowd, increasingly threatening and still swarming around the building, did not disperse, and nor did Lord George request that they should. It was not within his power to order people to obey him, he would later say: that authority lay elsewhere.

It was in fact the responsibility of Brackley Kennet, the Lord Mayor of London, to read the crowd the Riot Act, which declared any assembly of twelve or more people to be unlawful, and when called upon must disperse or face punishment. That he did not do so was remiss of him and his negligible grasp of the situation barely improved thereafter.

No doubt fuelled by alcohol (several gin houses had already been broken into) the mob now tried to force its way into the Parliament building, and a few MPs trying to enter or exit were dragged from their carriages and roughed up.

*The Times* newspaper reported:

> They attempted in like manner to force their way into the House of Peers but by the good management of Sir Francis Molyneux and the proper exertion of the doorkeepers the passages from the street door and around the House were kept open.
>
> About ten o'clock the mob made a parade in different directions from the Palace Yard where part of them went to the Roman Chapel in Lincolns-in-Field where they began to break down the doors, and then pulled down the rails, seats, pews, communion table brought them into the street, laid them against the doors and set fire to them. About eleven o'clock the Guards came, and much rioting ensued. They took several of the ringleaders prisoner but with the assistance of the mob they made good their escape.

The rioting spread rapidly and though much of the violence was random the homes of the rich and powerful soon became targets, with those of leading politicians such as the former and future prime minister the Marquis of Rockingham, the Duke of Devonshire, the hated Chief Magistrate, the Earl of Mansfield, and indeed Sir George Savile himself, being stoned and having their windows smashed. Some were even burned.

The violence did not relent over the coming days: if anything it became even more intense, with anything that could be identified as Catholic likely to be attacked and more than a hundred chapels and churches trashed, looted, and torched. Even foreign embassies such as the Sardinian and Bavarian were besieged as their residents cowered behind their walls in fear of their lives.

The absence of any visible authority on the streets (a small number of arrests were made by the thinly stretched and over-burdened Bow Street Runners, but most soon eluded their captors) allowed the mob to act with impunity and thirty-six major conflagrations were reported to have broken out in London, many at the same time, with little attempt to douse the flames other than by locals whose own homes were threatened.

Some of the worst rioting and violence occurred in the Moorfields district, one of the few areas of open land in London and home to a great many Catholic Irish immigrants. It was a place notorious for its brothels, taverns, and as a hiding place for highwaymen and those evading justice.

Aware they would serve as a magnet for the rioters, leading Catholics approached the Lord Mayor pleading for protection, but none was forthcoming. As the mob descended many fled, leaving their homes to be broken into and ransacked. Those who remained were likely to be beaten or subjected to public humiliation.

The mob rampaged through the streets of London virtually unchecked for five days and it wasn't until 7 June, when they converged upon and threatened to break into the Bank of England, that, following consultations with the king, Lord North at last ordered troops on to the streets to restore order. They could only do so by opening fire on the crowds and around 450 people were killed and 700 wounded.

The militia sent to defend the Bank of England was commanded by John Wilkes, the famous Radical MP who had himself ten years earlier been the darling of the mob. Now he too ordered his troops to open fire. His reputation never recovered.

The crowds dispersed over the next few days, leaving carnage behind them: shops looted, churches burned, homes ransacked, streets in ruins.

Soldiers Deployed, John Seymour Lucas (1789). (Public domain via Wikimedia Commons)

Some returned home nursing sore heads, others with broken bones and gunshot wounds. Others disappeared back into the London fog laden with booty; some never returned home at all.

In the immediate aftermath the Government dismissed the rioters as being the refuse of society and not true Englishmen: they were foreigners, gypsies, vagabonds, beggars, and thieves. Hundreds were arrested and twenty-five executed, including the Jew Samuel Solomon from Whitechapel and the black washerwoman Charlotte Gardiner, who were both hanged for demolishing a house; the street thug William Taplin, who extorted money with menaces in the name of the Protestant Association, he said, but in truth to line his own pockets; and the ex-soldier William MacDonald who had lost his arm in service to the Crown but was now hanged for damaging property.

But many of those subject to fines, deportation, terms of imprisonment and worse were respectable in their daily lives and as such less worthy of reporting.

Lord George Gordon, who had not participated in the riots even if some believed he had instigated them, was also arrested and arraigned at the Old Bailey charged with treason.

Incarcerated in the Tower of London, George was shown all the respect due to his rank. His cell was furnished to his liking, he ate regularly and well, and he was permitted visitors, among them the leading Methodist preacher John

Wesley. His connections also ensured that he had the best possible defence counsel, a close family friend, Lord Erskine, who successfully argued during the trial that in delivering a petition to Parliament for the consideration of its Members he could hardly be accused of committing a treasonable act, nor could he be held responsible for people whose behaviour he had had at no time incited or encouraged. He was acquitted of all charges.

The man who would be blamed was Brackley Kennet, the Lord Mayor of London, who had failed to respond sufficiently to events and was fined £1,000 for criminal negligence.

The riots had, to all intents and purposes, ended Lord George's political career, and over the next few years his behaviour became increasingly erratic. In 1786 he was excommunicated by the Archbishop of Canterbury for his refusal to appear as a witness before an ecclesiastical court and a year later he fled abroad to avoid arrest for alleged defamation. He was to return, but was '*apprehended in Birmingham in the garb of a Jew with a long beard and having undergone circumcision he had embraced the religion of the unbelievers.*'

Lord George was sentenced to five years' imprisonment, not for his conversion, but for a charge of defamation outstanding against him, which he strenuously denied.

Despite his erratic, some would later say insane, behaviour it still came as a surprise to discover that the former President of the Protestant Association and the man who had sparked the most serious anti-Catholic riots ever seen in England had converted to Judaism. Old friends and colleagues were genuinely shocked:

> Unknown to every class of man but those of the Jewish religion, among whom he has passed his time in the greatest cordiality and friendship... he also appears with a beard of extraordinary length, and the usual raiment of a Jew.

Lord George had not converted on a whim (he was never less than earnest), and in gaol he lived as an Orthodox Jew, following the dietary laws as best he could, often without success.

Many of those disappointed that they had lost their champion claimed that he had been bewitched by a Jewess he lived with while abroad, but for all his faults he was never less than sincere.

In January 1793 George was considered for release, but the court would not accept the testimony of the two Jews he had chosen to bear witness on his behalf. His family then offered to pay his bail, but Lord George refused their help, insisting that to pay for his release would be to admit his guilt, which he wouldn't do. As a result, he remained in prison where soon after he contracted typhoid fever.

On 1 November 1793, aged 42, Lord George Gordon, still professing the faith of his conversion, died. '*Such was the end of a man, once, perhaps, the most popular idol of the mob, and, for some days, the terror of all London.*'

# Chapter 2

# Luddites, Peterloo, and Captain Swing

On 11 May 1812, the Prime Minister Spencer Perceval was assassinated. He had been walking through the House of Commons lobby on his way to a meeting when John Bellingham approached him, shouted something, then shot him once through the chest. He died soon after.

The assassination stunned the nation. No British prime minister had ever been murdered before and the fear quickly spread that it was a prelude to revolution. It was in fact no such thing; Bellingham was no blood-soaked radical, but a disgruntled businessman who had been the subject of a false arrest and had since seen all his petitions for compensation rejected. Nevertheless, the event sent a shudder down the spine of the British Establishment.

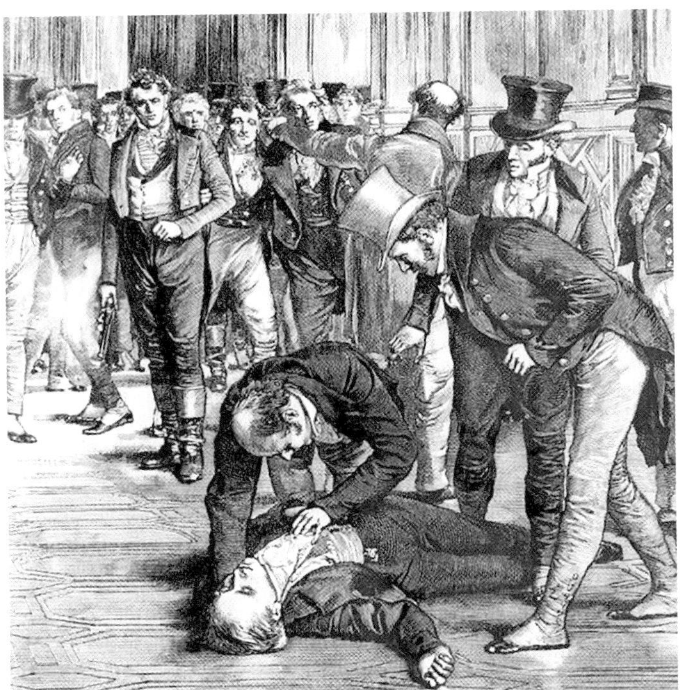

The Assassination of Spencer Perceval. (Alchetron.com)

In the wake of Perceval's murder, a new administration was formed under Lord Liverpool, who was determined to restore order and maintain the status quo. He created a spy network to root out radicalism and even more controversially employed agent provocateurs to create situations whereby the harshest punishment of the law could be brought to bear upon potential miscreants. It also regularly deployed troops to crush any semblance of opposition. Taking a hard line on all dissent made it quite clear that the government would take all measures to defend the interests of the merchants, the landed aristocracy, and the propertied classes.

In the first decade of the nineteenth century Britain had been under serious threat of invasion from Napoleonic France. The surge of patriotism that this provoked, and the abiding public interest in the affairs of the British Army fighting overseas, papered over the cracks at a time of growing social tension at home, but as French power began to wane, and the Napoleonic Wars neared their end, these social tensions once more came to the fore.

In 1812, unrest among the weavers of the East Midlands and the West Riding of Yorkshire led to disorder and acts of machine-breaking. Those responsible soon earned the name Luddites after the mythical King Ned Ludd, in whose name they signed off their letters of intimidation.

Luddism was a protest by a skilled workforce against the depressed income, reduced circumstances and rising unemployment caused by the introduction of machine technology, and not merely the byword for backward-thinking mindless destruction it has since become. The Luddites were well organised, with many of them members of what were at the time illegal trade unions, to which they swore an oath and collected subscription fees.

The Luddite attacks were carefully targeted, were only ever launched after warnings had been issued, and were carried out in secret. The participants' propensity for wearing women's clothes during their raids has never been fully explained, but it is fair to assume it was done for reasons of disguise, though it may also have been an act of contempt towards those they sought to intimidate.

Handloom weavers had prospered in the latter decades of the eighteenth century following technological innovations such as James Hargreaves's Spinning Jenny in 1765 and Richard Arkwright's water frame three years later, which had greatly increased the quantity of yarn produced. However, these advances in machine technology did not stop there. In 1785, Edmund Cartwright invented a weaving machine operated by a steam engine that could produce four times the amount of woven fabric in a day than a skilled handloom weaver. Moreover, it was so simple to use it could be operated by a child.

Cartwright's new power loom was not an instant success, but as more and more were introduced over the next few years it became increasingly apparent that the handloom weaver's days were numbered. As the larger cotton mills began power looms, the work available to the skilled handloom weavers diminished and unemployment rose accordingly, with those who could still find work earning wages little above subsistence level.

The handloom weavers began to fight back and in a three-week period during March 1811, more than 200 stocking frame machines were destroyed in Nottinghamshire alone, and the unrest spiralled. Over the next 12 months some 1,000 machines were destroyed, with attacks becoming a near nightly occurrence, and by the following year the unrest had spread to Yorkshire and Lancashire and had taken on more sinister overtones, with the advent of King Ludd and his secret army of armed Redeemers.

Warning letters were sent to mill owners stating that if they did not remove the machines from their factories then they should fear for their lives and those of their family. Mills were attacked in Stockport and Manchester; not only was machinery wrecked, but buildings were also burned to the ground, and the violence escalated as the same fate befell mill owner's homes and attempts were made on their lives. The reaction of the mill owners was not to seek compromise, but to employ armed guards for their own and their property's protection.

On 28 April 1812, the mill owner William Horsfall, who had been overheard to say that he would '*ride up his saddle in Luddite blood*' was intercepted on Crosland Moor near Huddersfield and shot dead by a young weaver named George Mellor.

Under pressure from the mill owners, many of whom sat in Parliament, the Government decided to take a hard line. More than 12,000 troops were sent to the area, rewards were offered for the capture and arrest of the Luddite ringleaders, and legislation was passed in Parliament making machine-wrecking a capital offence.

The attacks on the cotton mills continued, however, but with the introduction of the troops they invariably ended in fatalities. In the summer of 1812, eight men were sentenced to death at Lancashire Assizes and hanged, and a little later a further fifteen were executed in York and many others sentenced to transportation to Australia.

Such harsh and exemplary punishment eventually broke the back of the Luddites, and though sporadic attacks continued, by 1817 Luddite resistance had virtually ceased.

During that intervening five-year period the number of skilled artisan handloom weavers had been reduced from over 40,000 to less than 5,000. Those still working had also seen their wages more than halve from 21s a week to only 9s a week.

Though the Luddites never sought political revolution, it was a movement driven by the fear of unemployment and hunger: what the eminent Marxist historian E.P Thompson in his seminal work *The Making of the English Working Class* referred to as 'collective bargaining by riot'. However, there were other forces at work. It was the first indication that a crisis point had been reached in the social and productive relationships of the country. It heralded a sustained period of social unrest unprecedented in British history that has since become known as the 'Heroic Age of Popular Radicalism'.

The suppression of the Luddites wasn't the last time that the impoverished weavers tried to better their situation and have their case heard. Heeding the advice of radical speakers, they abandoned their campaign of violence and instead decided to travel to London and petition the Prince Regent directly. On 10 March 1817, 5,000 marchers gathered at St Peter's Field in Manchester.

The Government had recently introduced legislation outlawing large assemblies, so the marchers had decided to walk to London in groups of ten, with each man carrying a page of the petition with twenty names on. Each marcher also carried a blanket to sleep under at night, giving the protest its name, the March of the Blanketeers.

The intended march did not start well when the money that had been donated to feed the walkers on their journey was stolen. The Government also had no intention of permitting 5,000 men to gather support as they marched on the capital. The march was harassed almost from the time it left Manchester by local yeomanry, and very few of the marchers got further than Stockport, less than ten miles from their starting point.

Still the disturbances continued, and in the early hours of 10 June some 300 men, mostly unemployed stockingers and quarrymen, met in the village of Pentrich in Derbyshire. They were armed with pikes, knives, clubs, and a few antique muskets. They had gathered to be led on a march to Nottingham by Jeremiah Brandreth, a man of violent temper who had murder on his mind. He believed that a few exemplary deaths would incite revolution in the area and with mass support he could lead his men on an attack upon London and bring down the Government.

It was a miserable night, cold and pouring with rain, and many of the isolated farmhouses the men stopped at along the way for food and shelter bolted their doors to them: where was the support for their cause Brandreth had promised?

When a servant at a particular farmhouse refused to cooperate with the marchers Brandreth shot him dead. Appalled at the deed they had just witnessed, disappointed by the reception they had received, and discouraged by the weather, many of the men now began to desert. Brandreth threatened to shoot anyone else who tried to leave, but morale was by now so low that when they reached Nottingham, and a small squad of Hussars appeared on the horizon, the men simply threw down their weapons and fled.

Brandreth was arrested and, along with two other men, hanged for treason. It was alleged at the trial that a Government spy, Oliver, had really been behind the plan, but this has never been proved.

In 1815 the harsh conditions in the countryside were made even worse by the eruption of Mount Tambora in the Dutch East Indies, which sent volcanic ash high into the sky and across the globe, blotting out the sun for months in what became known as the 'Year without Summer.' The weather cycle was thrown into disarray and as temperatures plummeted the land could not be tilled, and those crops already sown invariably failed.

In the meantime, the end of the Napoleonic Wars in 1815 had already plunged Britain into a period of economic crisis. The subsequent drop in Government spending on war materiel depressed foreign markets and the return of thousands of demobilised troops and a series of failed harvests led to widespread unemployment. For example, in the Essex town of Halstead, of the population of 3,279, some 2,012 were in receipt of poor relief.

The growing feeling of discontent was only exacerbated by the passage of the Corn Laws that same year.

On 2 December 1816, people gathered at Spa Fields in London to protest living conditions. Their demands were the usual: cheaper bread and an extension of the franchise. It was the second such demonstration in less than a month. The first had passed off peacefully: this one would not, and neither was it intended to.

The demonstration had been organised by the Spenceans (followers of the radical Thomas Spence, who had died two years earlier) who were intent on the violent overthrow of the government and the destruction of the status quo, and the plans had been laid for just that.

Many of the 20,000 demonstrators who had assembled broke away and began to march in the direction of the Tower of London, where munitions intended for the army were stored, and they were in an ugly mood: a suspected government spy had already been stabbed to death, and a gun shop looted.

The authorities had been forewarned of the conspirators' intentions, however, and had deployed troops in the mob's path. The atmosphere was tense, but a volley of gunfire was all that was required to disperse them.

The Government was aware that despite the apparent spontaneity of many of the disturbances, that wasn't always the case. There was a radical underground active in the country, and the fear of a nationwide insurrection was real.

The 1790s had seen the emergence of 'Corresponding Societies', groupings of mostly better-off, better-educated working-class artisans and tradesmen who largely supported the ideas of the French Revolution.

The Government, which feared the importation of ideas that had seen the aristocracy not only lose their positions of power, but also their heads, was quick to suppress the activities of the Corresponding Societies, but it was to prove far more difficult to eradicate the idea, and the radical press continued to grow in support and influence.

William Cobbett, the son of a farmer, a prickly and difficult character who had previously served in the army and was conservative by nature, had turned to the cause of radical reform after witnessing first-hand the extreme poverty and starvation that bedevilled his beloved countryside. In January 1802 he published his 'Political Register', which he used to criticise the Government of William Pitt the Younger, and was later to cleverly circumvent the punitive Stamp Duty by publishing it as a weekly pamphlet at only two pennies a copy. His critics lampooned it as the *Tu'penny Trash*, but Cobbett embraced the name with glee, and it soon acquired a circulation of over 40,000 a week and was widely distributed. It was to become not only a mouthpiece for radical reform, but the first working-class opinion former.

In 1828 Cobbett supported the cause of Catholic Emancipation and in 1830 published his *Rural Rides*, a graphic description of the scenes of neglect, hunger, and poverty he witnessed as he travelled around rural England. By 1832 he had turned his attentions to campaigning for the extension of the franchise to include the working class and an end to the corruption in electoral politics.

Cobbett is a difficult man to assess: his generosity of spirit towards the working man and the poor in general did not extend to the Jews, for whom he had a deep personal loathing, and he fell out with his friend William Wilberforce over his role in the abolition of the slave trade and his support for the '*fat and lazy* and *laughing and singing negroes*', as he referred to them.

Unlike many of his radical colleagues William Cobbett was never a revolutionary. Indeed, the language of much of the radical press did not always reflect the attitudes of its readership or intended readership. For example, Thomas Wooler, writing in *Black Dwarf* stressed the right of people to violently resist oppression, if necessary: always, and in all circumstances. While Richard Carlile in *The Republican* even suggested that regicide might be the answer. But most people, it seemed, just wanted security of labour and be able to put food on the table.

The radical press however, had a broader agenda, and it was awash with references to rebellion and revolution.

In 1812, the Hampden Club was formed. It was made up of prominent Whig politicians and leading members of the more moderate wing of the Radical Movement. Its stated aim, regardless of the unrest in the countryside and the growing sense of discontent in the rapidly growing industrial towns, was to alleviate the situation through parliamentary reform. They did not seek social upheaval and revolution: indeed, they shrank at the very thought of it.

This was never going to be enough for the people who were tired of asking their betters to do right by them. Even so, they thought they could foster working-class support for their reformist agenda. However, when the radical Major John Cartwright went on a speaking tour of the Luddite areas, he was frequently heckled and effectively ostracised by those he believed he represented. The Hampden Club, however, was a sign of things to come.

The violence of many of the disturbances, the utterances of some of the radical journals, and the slogans of some of the protesters, such as 'Bread or Blood', frightened many in the radical movement as well as the Government.

At a conference held in London in 1817, even people considered ultra-radicals, such as Henry 'Orator' Hunt and Samuel Bamford, only went so far as to call for Manhood Suffrage and the Secret Ballot. William Cobbett did not even go this far, and advocated a property franchise. He was later to distance himself from the Hampden Club, feeling it was damaging his reputation with the poor.

Much of the Radical Movement was inherently conservative and the tactics of petitioning the ruling monarch, lobbying parliament, and looking to newly enriched industrialists for moral and financial support, emphasised this fact. However, there was no end to the violence.

On 16 August 1819, as many as 60,000 people massed in St Peter's Field, Manchester, to attend a meeting organised by the Patriotic Union to call for parliamentary reform.

The crowd eagerly anticipated the address of the meeting's star turn, Henry 'Orator' Hunt, so-called because of his fiery rhetoric and ability to rouse a crowd. Prior to the meeting the secretary of the Patriotic Union, Joseph Johnson, had written to Hunt:

> Nothing but ruin and starvation stare one in the face, the state of this district is truly terrible, and I believe that nothing, but the greatest exertion can prevent an insurrection. If only you in London were ready for it.

Unknown to Johnson and Hunt, this letter had been intercepted by Government spies and was interpreted as being an incitement to riot. Expecting trouble, the Government despatched the 15th Hussars to Manchester.

At 1pm Henry Hunt arrived at St Peter's Field in his trademark white top hat. It made him easily distinguishable, and the crowd erupted at the sight of him. Witnessing the reception afforded him the local magistrates, worried about how the crowd would respond should he be permitted to speak, issued a warrant for his arrest. Sixty mounted troops of the Manchester Yeomanry were ordered to force a way through the crowd to deliver the warrant and take Hunt into custody.

It was a swelteringly hot day, and tempers became quickly frayed as the yeomen pushed and barged their way through the thronging crowd, riding rough-shod over people in their way. The people responded angrily, and the poorly trained yeomanry came under a hail of bricks and bottles as attempts were made by some to unhorse them, and they began to panic as the crowd pressed in around them. Witnessing the scene from a house nearby, the chief magistrate, William Hutton, ordered the 15th Hussars to assist the Yeomanry and try to restore order, but the crowd was so tightly packed it was unable to disperse.

Seeing their colleagues in the yeomanry isolated and under threat, the Hussars charged with sabres drawn. Now the crowd did disperse, and in the panic eleven people were killed and more than 600 injured, some from sabre thrusts but most trampled underfoot. The radical press named it the Peterloo Massacre, a satirical reference to the Duke of Wellington's great victory at Waterloo three years earlier. They were outraged, a reaction only made worse by the Prince Regent's fulsome praise for the actions of those charged with policing the demonstration.

The fallout from the Peterloo Massacre was extensive, then but little changed as a result, at least in the short term.

Peterloo Massacre, Richard Carlile (1819). (Manchester Libraries)

Arthur Thistlewood was an ex-army officer who had embraced revolutionary ideals while resident in America and France. He was known to be an argumentative man, of whom it was said that he enjoyed a fight, verbal or otherwise.

Thistlewood had been arrested (but later released) following the Spa Fields Riot, but during his time in captivity three tickets for a journey to America valued at £180 had been taken from him. He wrote to the Home Secretary Lord Sidmouth demanding either their return or that suitable recompense be paid to him. When he received no reply, he challenged Lord Sidmouth to a duel. For this breach of the peace he was sentenced to a further 12 months, but still he sent a stream of letters complaining of the harsh conditions in which he was being kept.

This was the kind of man Thistlewood was: confrontational and determined to fight it out. He was considered too extreme by many of the leading radicals, who steadily distanced themselves from him.

Upon learning from a notification in *The Times* newspaper that much of the Cabinet would be dining at Lord Harrowby's house the following night, Thistlewood immediately laid a plan to attack the house and murder all the Cabinet members present. So enthused were some of his conspiratorial cabal at the prospect of the attack that one of them, a butcher named James Ings, vowed to decapitate each and every one of them and exhibit their severed heads on Westminster Bridge.

Thistlewood sent one of the conspirators, Jamaican-born William Davidson, who had previously worked as a servant at Lord Harrowby's, to use his contacts there to garner further information. Davidson returned later that night and informed Thistlewood that as far as his contacts were aware Lord Harrowby was not even in London. Thistlewood concluded from this that Davidson had been deliberately misled: the attack would go ahead as planned.

Unknown to Thistlewood, his co-conspirator and friend George Edwards was in fact a government spy, and the notification in *The Times* was a falsification that had been used to flush the conspirators out. Thistlewood had been hoodwinked.

The following day he and eight other men gathered in the hayloft of a stable in Cato Street to prepare for the attack. He had recruited twenty-seven men, and he delayed for a time hoping others would turn up, but they never did.

Across the road, in the Horse and Groom public house, were Magistrate Richard Birney and twelve Bow Street Runners. They were waiting for a unit of Coldstream Guards under the command of Lieutenant Lord Frederick FitzClarence. When they failed to turn up Birney, fearing he would lose his quarry, decided to go ahead and try to apprehend the conspirators without their assistance.

At around 7.30 in the evening the Bow Street Runners, led by George Ruthven (Magistrate Birney had decided not to make the arrest himself, and instead waited outside), burst into the stable, quickly overcoming James Ings who had been left on guard. The other conspirators, hearing the commotion, desperately tried to arm their pistols, but there was too little time. With swords drawn there was a short but fierce mêlée, during which Thistlewood ran one Bow Street Runner through, killing him.

Most of the conspirators, including Davidson, were taken at the scene, but Thistlewood and a few others managed to escape. They were too well known to the authorities to remain at liberty for long, however, and they were arrested soon after.

At their subsequent trial for high treason William Davidson was by far the most eloquent of the defendants. In one famous exchange with the presiding judge, he doubted the likelihood of his getting a fair trial:

Arrest of the Cato Street Conspirators (1820), unknown author. (Public domain via Wikimedia Commons)

> You may suppose that because I am a man of colour, I am without understanding or feeling and would act the brute. I am not one of that sort and when not employed in my business, I have employed myself as a teacher of Sunday School.

The judge replied:

> You may rest perfectly assured that with respect to the colour of your countenance, no prejudice either has, or will exist in any part of this Court against you, a man of colour is entitled to British justice as much as the fairest British subject.

Davidson may have received a fair trial, but he was convicted nonetheless and after he was sentenced to be hanged, he made a final statement to the court:

> It is an ancient custom to resist tyranny... would you not rather govern a country of spirited men, than cowards? I can die but once in this world, and the only regret is, that I have a large family of small children, and when I think of that, it unmans me.

Arthur Thistlewood had said little throughout his trial, accepting his fate with his usual defiance. His last words on the scaffold were: '*I shall soon know the grand secret.*'

The realisation dawned on the Government, and the landed oligarchy in whose interests it was mostly run, that the people could not be kept down by coercion and force indefinitely: something had to be done. Likewise, the Radical Movement became aware that violence only begat violence, and that it was the Government which had the soldiers, the sabres, the muskets, and the cannon.

Though the discontent remained, and the disturbances continued, violent radicalism waned in the wake of the Peterloo Massacre and the fate of the Cato Street Conspirators. Most of the energy of the Radical Movement now went into the cause of electoral reform and the ending of 'Old Corruption'.

However, there was to be one more major eruption of widespread violence that served to emphasise the need for change.

In the summer of 1830, riots broke out in East Kent that took a form that was reminiscent of the Luddism of fifteen years before.

Developments in agricultural husbandry and the increased use of machine technology made farming less labour-intensive, and many poor labourers, who had previously struggled to subsist on what was often only seasonal work, now found they had no work at all and their situation was made worse by the escalation in the rate of enclosures, or the privatisation of the common land that had been used for centuries by the poor to graze livestock or grow a little produce for themselves and their families. During hard times it had often been the use of the common land that had spared the labourers from the prospect of starvation.

The increased unemployment and consequent hunger were not sufficiently relieved by the wholly inadequate system of poor relief, which was paid for by the wealthier taxpayers of any parish. They were reluctant to provide for those they considered to be the idle poor, who rendered no service for the money they received. As the number of people unable to find gainful employment increased, so did the burden upon those who could.

The most obvious symbol of the agricultural workers' impoverishment was the steam-powered threshing machine, and hundreds were smashed over the next few months as the protests spread across the south-east of England. Hayricks were burned, as were barns, and letters of intimidation were sent to employers, this time signed in the name of the mythical 'Captain Swing'.

Parish priests were also the target of threats because of the tithe that entitled the Church of England to 10 per cent of the parish harvest, levied across all the agricultural workers in the parish regardless of their ability to pay. This at one time could have been paid in kind through goods or labour, but was now exclusively a cash levy.

Unlike the Luddites, however, the Captain Swing protesters did not disguise themselves, but descended on wealthy farmers in their hundreds in broad daylight to negotiate settlements. Intimidated by the labourers, most farmers agreed to their demands, though many reneged on them later.

Once again, the Government's response was swift and brutal, and more than 2,000 farm labourers were arrested and brought to trial. Many were sentenced to transportation and terms of imprisonment, while nineteen were hanged.

It was obvious to most that such disturbances could not be allowed to continue, and some form of reform had to be contemplated. The prime minister, the Duke of Wellington, disagreed, believing the British system of government to be the ideal. His refusal to move on the issue led to the windows of the hero of Waterloo's London home, Apsley House, being smashed. On 15 November 1830, Wellington's Tory administration fell and he was forced to resign.

The new Whig prime minister, Earl Grey, unlike his predecessor, was quick to recognise that a people who had traditionally been governed by deference and consent could not be forced to comply at the point of a bayonet. He was no less a believer in the British system of government than his predecessor had been, but, fearing for its future, he wished to ensure its preservation even in a modified form if necessary. He determined upon a cause of reform.

The Reform Act Grey proposed had the support of the Radical Movement and his own Whig supporters in the House of Commons, but was vehemently opposed by most Tories, especially in the House of Lords.

Grey's first attempt to pass the Reform Bill was defeated in the House of Commons and as a result he requested that the king dissolve Parliament so that he could take the issue to the country. In the ensuing election the Whigs were returned with an overwhelming majority and in September 1831 the Bill was once more put to a Commons vote, where it was passed with a majority of more than 100. However, there remained little prospect of it passing in the House of Lords, which at the time had the same right to reject proposed legislation as the House of Commons.

The Bill, as expected, was easily defeated by forty-one votes and the margin would have been even greater had some Tory Lords not abstained from the vote, wanting to avoid controversy and potential trouble on their country estates if they were seen to oppose it. The Lords Spiritual, the bishops representing the Church of England, had no such scruples and voted twenty-two to one against the Bill.

The night that the Reform Bill was rejected the people erupted in fury and scenes of violence were witnessed the length and breadth of the country. There were large-scale riots in Nottingham and Derby, counties such as Dorset, Somerset, and Leicestershire became almost ungovernable, and in Bristol jails were broken into, prisoners freed, shops looted, and the bishop's residence destroyed. The country houses of some lords were also attacked, and attempts made to set them alight.

The Radical Movement was also busy organising a campaign to withhold payment of tax and encouraging people to withdraw their savings from the Bank of England, causing a run on the pound, and once more there was talk of not bothering with reform at all but of simply abolishing the aristocracy and the monarchy altogether.

Considering the impossibility of any Reform Bill ever being passed in the House of Lords, Grey requested that King William IV create 100 new Whig peers to secure its passage. The king shrank from taking such drastic action to guarantee legislation that he was personally opposed to. He refused to adopt the measure and Earl Grey had little choice but to resign.

The king now turned to the one man he knew he could trust and who he knew would not compromise on the issue of reform, the Duke of Wellington. But with the country in uproar, even he recognised the hopelessness of the situation and offered some mild reform, but it was too little too late. Amid the pandemonium he was obliged to inform the king that there was nothing he could do and resigned once more. King William now had little choice but to reappoint Earl Grey and yield to his demands.

Still reluctant to create any new Whig peers, let alone a hundred, the king first wrote to all the leading Tory lords. He did not want to lose the inbuilt pro-monarchy Tory majority in the House of Lords, and neither did they. Once his intentions had been made clear they consented to the passage of the Bill which received royal assent on 7 June 1832.

The Great Reform Act of 1832 was first and foremost a recognition that things had to change, but it was more radical in intent than it ever was in deed. Rotten Boroughs, political placemen, and parliamentary sinecures were effectively abolished and the urban conurbations that were springing up, the result of the Industrial Revolution, were to be represented in the House of Commons for the first time. The extension of the franchise was slight, however, increasing the number of eligible male voters from around 400,000 to 650,000, or one in six of the adult male population.

The franchise was to be extended again in 1867 to include most urban workers and by 1884 most agricultural labourers.

Women, however, were excluded from the franchise until the passage of the Representation of the Peoples Act 1918, eighty-six years after the initial Reform Act and not on the same terms with men until ten years later.

The widespread disturbances in the early decades of the nineteenth century and the radical politics they both engendered and reflected had made the country close to ungovernable. The fear that Britain would follow France on the road to revolution was real, and the shadow of the guillotine terrified those in positions of power who saw themselves as the most likely victims.

The 1832 Reform Act was the first recognition that Britain needed to be a country that was governed with the consent of its people as expressed through the ballot box and not just a fiefdom run in the interests of a propertied elite whose wishes were imposed at the point of a bayonet or at the end of a hangman's noose.

# Chapter 3

# Jacobites

*'Speed, bonnie boat, like a bird on a wing*
*Onward! The sailors cry;*
*Carry the lad that's born to be king.*
*Over the sea to Skye.'*

Charles Edward Louis John Casimir Silvester Severino Maria Stuart, better known to history as Bonnie Prince Charlie, was born in Rome on 31 December 1720. He was the son of the Stuart claimant to the English throne, James Francis Edward Stuart. His mother, Maria Clementina Sobieski, was the granddaughter of the Polish King John III. Thus Charles was not just of Scottish blood, but also of Polish ancestry. Raised in the Eternal City, he was culturally, intellectually, and temperamentally an Italian.

Charles's father, the 'Old Pretender', was the son of the last Stuart King of England James II, who had been deposed by William Prince of Orange in 1688. Since the old king's death, he had made several attempts to regain the throne for his family. In 1708, a delay in setting out caused by an attack of measles saw the Royal Navy prevent him from landing in Scotland. He tried again in 1715, but despite a battle being fought at Sheriffmuir, which saw both sides claim victory, he was so disappointed by the response of the Highland clans to the possibility of a Stuart restoration that he left a terse note telling his supporters to look to themselves and took ship back to France.

Once safely back on the Continent, James established a court in exile, but his attempts at open rebellion had come to an end. In December 1743 he named his son Charles Prince Regent and gave him full authority to re-establish the Stuart dynasty in whatever way he thought best. Charles, the 'Young Pretender', took his charge seriously and for a martial prince this meant honourably by force of arms. It seemed not to trouble him that he had no arms and no army.

On 23 July 1745, the soon-to-be 'Bonnie Prince' landed on the Isle of Eriskay in the Hebrides with just seven companions. He had little to offer

Bonnie Prince Charlie (1745), Allan Ramsay. (Public domain via Wikimedia Commons)

the Highlanders in return for their support, just the desire, he said, to make Scotland happy and the promise of a French army to come.

The venture was foolhardy to say the least, and the initial response to his arrival appeared to reflect that. This was less than enthusiastic, with many of the clan chieftains reluctant to rally to his cause. But Charlie was a Stuart, a Catholic and, at just 25 years of age, full of manly vigour. He also had agents working on his behalf, and by the time he raised his standard at Glenfinnan on 19 August 1745, some 1,200 men of the MacDonald, MacDonnell and Cameron clans had pledged themselves to his cause.

The prince continued to gather support as he advanced south and met little, if any, resistance. He easily captured the towns of Coatbridge and Perth and on 11 September he occupied Edinburgh, though he was unable to capture its castle. On 21 September the Jacobites, as they were known, encountered the only Hanoverian army in Scotland of any note.

Sir John Cope, with 2,500 men, had set up camp near the town of Prestonpans. He was an experienced and energetic soldier, but conventional in his thinking. He had expected to meet the Jacobites on the field of battle when both armies had formed up in the normal way.

However, Sir George Murray, the ablest of the Jacobite commanders, had ordered a forced march at night, which enabled the Jacobite army to emerge out of the mist and attack without warning at first light. Sir John Cope was taken completely by surprise and the Hanoverians, with sleep still in their eyes and reduced to abject terror by the blood-curdling cries of a full-bloodied Highland charge, broke and fled in panic. In the rout that followed more than 400 were killed and a further 1,500 taken prisoner. The only Hanoverian army in Scotland had been destroyed for the cost of just thirty Jacobites killed and seventy wounded.

General Cope was later cleared of negligence at a court martial, but with his reputation in tatters he was quick to blame the men under his command, declaring his English soldiers too scared to stand up to the ferocious Highlanders and that his successor in Scotland would fare no better than he had. It mattered little for the time being: Scotland belonged to the Bonnie Prince.

For five weeks the prince remained in Edinburgh, receiving letters of congratulation and delegations of well-wishers, but little practical support. Scotland may have been his, but its people were not, and many remained sceptical or openly hostile. All this would change once he regained the throne for his father, he believed. At a heated council of war, he argued vehemently that the Jacobite army must invade England itself, that the Hanoverians were in disarray, and that as their best troops were away fighting in Flanders, London lay open. He had also received reports that Tories in England were preparing to flock to his banner and that a French invasion was imminent. It was he said, now or never.

Lord George Murray was sceptical that any such support would materialise in England or France, and argued instead that the prince should remain in Scotland and ensure himself of its support first. The point at issue was a stark one: consolidate what they already had, or risk everything they had gained on the throw of a dice. There was little room for manoeuvre and the two men and their supporters argued late into the night. In the end the prince got his way, but only by one vote.

On 3 November 1745, the Jacobite army, only 6,000 strong but expecting to rally support on the march south, set out for London. The news sent the capital into a panic as people fled the city, shops were boarded up, there was a run on the pound and preparations were made should the king need to make a hasty departure. Yet for all the nervousness in London and elsewhere about the prospect of a Stuart restoration, there was little real threat. Support for the Jacobite cause was slight, the English Tories did not rally to the prince's cause as expected, and only in Manchester did some 250 disgruntled Episcopalians join the Scots army. Despite popular loathing of the Hanoverian monarchy there was little enthusiasm for a Catholic Stuart on the throne of England.

Despite the indifference of the people to the Jacobite cause, and its army being further diminished by having to leave garrisons at Manchester and Carlisle, the advance continued south deep into hostile country with no hope of reinforcement. The army's position became more perilous with every advance, as the Hanoverians had not been slow to respond. General Wade was in hot pursuit from the north-east, the army of the king's youngest son the Duke of Cumberland barred the route to London, and the city itself had been transformed into an armed camp.

Only the masterful manoeuvring of his forces by Lord George Murray allowed the Jacobites to evade the various traps that had been laid for them, and by 4 December they had reached the town of Derby, just 125 miles from London. But Murray was also convinced that they were heading for disaster, and demanded another council of war, where serious questions were raised. Where was the support of the English Tories? Where was the promised French invasion?

The prince was forced to admit that his assurances had been so much hot air, but he insisted that once London was reached the French invasion would surely come. Lord George Murray argued otherwise and claimed that in London they would be trapped by superior forces with more arriving all the time from the Continent. Worse still, their route back to Scotland would be cut off. This time the Clan leaders ignored the impassioned pleas of their prince and voted unanimously to return to the Highlands. Denied what he believed to be his destiny, the prince threw a tantrum and sulked on his horse all the way back to the border.

Once again, through a series of brilliant feints, Lord George Murray was able to evade the pursuers, but he was forced to abandon the garrisons at Manchester and Carlisle to their fate. They suffered grievously as a result.

Lord George and the other Clan leaders now tried to persuade the prince to abandon his dream of a Stuart restoration in England and instead establish himself as king of an independent Scotland. But in this Charles had little interest: he had sought to use Scotland as a stepping-stone to recapturing England for his father, which he knew could not be achieved without the support of the Clans. Frustrated, he forced the city of Glasgow to replenish his army and wasted men and resources on a pointless siege of Stirling Castle.

In the meantime, the Hanoverian army in Scotland had been reinforced to 7,000 men and had a new commander in Sir Henry Hawley. He saw the prince's siege of Stirling Castle as an opportunity to attack the distracted Jacobite army, but Lord George Murray reacted first. He knew the 67-year-old Sir Henry to be an arrogant and complacent man with a liking for the bottle, who was unlikely to have made adequate preparations. So, adopting tactics similar to those he had used at Prestonpans, he once more unleashed his Highlanders early in the morning upon the still slumbering Hanoverians.

Hawley, who had housed himself some 2,000 yards behind his army's encampment, at first refused to believe that the Jacobite army was upon him. When he did at last react it was too late, as, leading his cavalry in a counterattack, eighty dragoons were killed in the first volley of gunfire and the rest quickly fled, riding over the Glasgow Regiment that was following close behind. However, unlike at Prestonpans not all the Hanoverian troops fled from the terrifying Highland charge and Hawley was able to extricate his army intact, although in some disarray.

Yet again Lord George Murray had won a great victory, with the Hanoverians losing more than 350 killed and 300 captured for the loss of just fifty Highlanders with a further eighty wounded. But at Falkirk the English had not run away.

The prince, who was by this time refusing even to acknowledge let alone speak to Lord George, did not try to press home his advantage but instead continued the pointless siege of Stirling Castle.

Sir Henry Hawley was removed from command of the Hanoverian forces in Scotland and replaced by the Duke of Cumberland, who had brought his own army north to complete the task of destroying the Jacobite threat once and for all.

Criticised for failing to exploit the opportunity provided by Lord George's victory at Falkirk to eliminate the Hanoverian presence in Scotland, the prince decided to take sole and complete command of his army, declaring that there would be no more councils of war. Either the clans followed him, or they did not.

Increasingly disenchanted with the clan chieftains, the prince turned to the Irish in his entourage for advice, in particular Adjutant-General Walter O'Sullivan, who chose Drumrossie Moor near Culloden as the place to confront Cumberland's army.

This was clearly a mistake, and the clan leaders knew it. But the prince was no longer listening to them. The terrain at Culloden could barely have suited Cumberland better: its low stone walls provided cover for his troops, while the open and treeless ground beyond provided a wide arc of delivery for his artillery and was perfect for cavalry, of which the Jacobites had none. The clans would also be attacking uphill, which would only serve to negate the ferocity of the Highland charge.

The clan leaders begged the prince not to give battle at Culloden and some suggested that his own liking for the bottle was clouding his judgement. But the prince would have none of it. He said he would '*trust in God*'.

On the night of 15 April 1746, the Hanoverian encampment resounded to music and much merriment as the troops celebrated the Duke of Cumberland's birthday. Extra rations had been distributed and the rum flowed freely at the duke's expense. The soldiery were relaxed and happy, making Lord George Murray believe it the perfect opportunity to repeat the success of Prestonpans. With a forced night march his men could fall upon the Hanoverian camp at first light before it had even awoken, let alone sobered up.

Despite their mutual antipathy, which meant them having to communicate through a third party, the prince decided to give the go-ahead to this plan.

Because of the failings of Walter O'Sullivan, who as quartermaster had done nothing to secure the food supply, many of the Highlanders had not eaten for days. They were cold, dishevelled and weak from hunger, and now they had to complete a forced march in the dead of night in wet, freezing conditions before fighting a battle.

The hastily arranged march soon descended into chaos as tired men, wet through and frozen, stumbled over one another in the darkness or became stuck in the mud and disappeared into bogs. By the time they arrived at the Hanoverian camp it was already daylight and the troops were awake, armed, and going about their business. Lord George had no choice but to abandon the attack and march his men straight back to where they had come from.

The following day, 16 April, the Duke of Cumberland marched his troops onto Drumrossie Moor and the Jacobites, many of them still exhausted from the march of the previous night, lined up to meet them.

Lord George Murray, fearing the worst, had reinforced the Jacobite army with 800 men of the Écossais Royaux (Royal Scots) and Irish piquets, exiled supporters of the Stuart claim to the throne, who had experience of fighting in the French army. These men would be held in reserve to cover the withdrawal he thought inevitable.

The Jacobites fired first, but their artillery barrage was short, ineffective, and quickly silenced. The Hanoverian artillery, in contrast, was deadly.

The gunners had years of experience fighting in Flanders and for thirty minutes fire raked the Jacobite lines, cutting swathes in the ranks. Impotent in the face of the barrage, the clan chiefs begged the prince to order the charge. From far behind the front line he refused, insisting that he wanted the Hanoverians to break formation first. This was to be a costly mistake, for in that short thirty minutes more than 500 Highlanders were cut down.

Frustrated, and unwilling to take any further needless casualties, some of the clans began to advance of their own accord. Seeing this, the prince at last gave the order for the charge to begin, but with some already engaging the enemy it was too late to organise the full-on rush of a Highland charge. However, even sporadic and uncoordinated it remained a sight to behold and terrifying to those forced to face it.

Clan Chattan, which had been the first to attack, had been halted by grapeshot and the men desperately scrambled to find cover where they could. Meanwhile, the MacDonald clan, which was traditionally positioned in the centre of the line, the place of greatest honour in any clan battle formation, had been moved to the left. Offended by the insult, they refused to charge at all. Meanwhile, the left flank of the Hanoverian army was hit hard, with the brunt of the attack being taken by two regiments of foot, Barrell's and DeJean's.

In no time at all Barrell's line was broken and his regiment smashed. He had lost seventeen men killed, 103 wounded, and the colours had been taken. Likewise, DeJean had suffered fourteen killed and sixty-eight wounded in a matter of minutes, and his line was close to disintegration. Seeing his left flank on the point of fracture and in danger of collapsing in on itself, the Duke of Cumberland was quick to react. He immediately filled the gaps in the rapidly thinning ranks with the 1,000 men of Semphill's Brigade. Among these was the regiment of Major James Wolfe, the future Hero of Quebec.

The Duke of Cumberland was marshalling his troops well and despite the ferocity of the Highland charge the Jacobites had been unable to make a breakthrough. Their last hope lay with the MacDonalds. Addressing them directly, the prince begged them to participate in the battle and eventually they agreed, but they did so reluctantly. When their charge came it was half-hearted and stopped short of the Hanoverian lines, where, keeping their distance, they jeered at the English and exchanged gunfire but refused to come into contact with them. Eventually, under intense fire, they broke and began to flee the field. Witnessing the flight of the MacDonalds, Lord George Murray brought forward the Écossais Royaux and Irish piquets, who exchanged volley fire with the Hanoverians, but were unable to stop the Highland retreat from becoming a rout.

The prince now rode among his fleeing troops, begging them to remain and fight. '*For God, for your Prince,*' he cried, but to no avail. Finally, he was escorted from the field, but as he departed a clan leader was heard to shout '*That's it, run you cowardly Italian.*'

The Battle of Culloden had been lost, but not necessarily the Jacobite cause. Despite the high casualties, with 1,500 killed, 1,000 wounded and 157 captured, a third of the Jacobite army had not been present at Culloden. Hanoverian casualties in contrast were relatively light, with just fifty killed and 259 wounded.

Some of the clans tried to rally after Culloden and some 1,500 men gathered at Ruthven Barracks to await orders, with others on the way. They believed they could still sustain a guerrilla campaign in the Highlands. Instead, they received an order from the prince that echoed the terse message sent by his father thirty years earlier: '*All is lost and each man must shift for himself as best he can.*' With no direction, and shorn of leadership, the clan army dispersed.

In the days immediately following the battle of Culloden, Cumberland's troops scoured the battlefield looking for wounded Scots to kill. He had fortified their resolve for the slaughter by telling them that the Jacobites had ordered that no quarter should be given, though no proof of any such order has ever been found.

In the meantime, the prince had made his way to Arisaig on the west coast of Scotland, from where he took ship to the island of Benbecula in the Hebrides. With a £30,000 price on his head, government troops in hot pursuit, at a loss about what to do and frequently drunk, he became utterly reliant upon the kindness of others.

A Jacobite loyalist, Flora MacDonald, now came to his rescue. Disguising Charlie as her Irish maid Betty Burke, she took him into her household before procuring a boat to take him to the Isle of Skye, from where, on 19 September 1746, he managed to take a ship which ferried him to safety in France. The prince left behind a weakened country with the last tribal society in western Europe destroyed.

Whereas most of Scotland celebrated Bonnie Prince Charlie's defeat, the Highlands were left devastated as families were cleared from the land and their homes destroyed. Those Jacobites taken prisoner, 3,741 of them, were sent south to stand trial. Of these 120 were executed, 648 remain unaccounted for, and 936 were transported to the colonies as indentured slaves. Most of the rest, including Flora MacDonald, were released in the general amnesty of 1747.

The captured clan leaders endured the fate reserved for traitors: to be hung, drawn, and quartered on Tower Hill.

Meanwhile, the Duke of Cumberland's exacting elimination of Jacobitism and the Highland Clearances that were to follow in the decades to come earned him the eternal enmity of the Highland Scots and the nickname 'Butcher Cumberland'.

Following his return to mainland Europe, the Bonnie Prince very soon ceased to be quite so bonnie. Increasingly irascible and bad-tempered, frequently mired in scandal, and drinking too much, he quickly became an embarrassment. Further attempts to raise a French invasion and restore the Stuart monarchy foundered thanks to the prince's habitual drunkenness. So dissolute was he that when his father died in 1766, Pope Clement XIII refused to bestow on him son the title of King of England, Scotland, and Ireland as expected.

Bonnie Prince Charlie, the heir to the Stuart dynasty, spent his final years in Rome drinking, whoring, and complaining that he had been betrayed by the cowardice of the Highland clans. By the end of his life he was a physical ruin, in some ways a mirror to the devastation caused to Scotland as a result of his attempts to defeat the Hanoverians.

## Part Eight

# Empire and Glory

# Chapter 1

# Clive of India

The idea of an England far from its own shores began during the reign of Elizabeth I, when thievery at sea alone failed to satisfy a queen always in want of flattery. It became more muscular during the Commonwealth and gained momentum with the growth of a navy that was the envy of the world. In relatively short time the British Empire became the largest the world has ever seen, spreading across a quarter of the globe (and this despite losing the American colony during the reign of George III). Yet there was no masterplan, no organising genius or guiding hand: merely a spirit of adventure, the persuasiveness of armed force, and the conviction that where England went the benefits of, Christianity, commerce and civilisation would follow. Few at the time doubted that they were doing right by their conquests, and so, with God on their side, a pistol at their hip, a map in their hand, and a contract in their pocket, they went, they saw, and they conquered. It was an empire of chance, or at least those chances taken by ruthless and unscrupulous opportunists, such as Robert Clive: Clive of India.

As a young man Clive had been a bully and a thug and in later life he was accused of venality and corruption. He was also a clever, audacious, resourceful, and courageous man, who against seemingly impossible odds single-handedly snatched for Britain what was to become the jewel in the crown of its burgeoning empire.

Born in 1725 in Styche, a small village near the town of Market Drayton in Shropshire, Robert Clive was from an old and well-established family of the Shires where his father, a lawyer, had for many years been the respected Member of Parliament.

It became clear early on, however, that Robert was not cast from the same mould. Rather, he was a young man on the make, who despite being raised in some comfort in a manor house was determined to make his own fortune, a fortune that could never be too great. He was a delinquent, a tearaway, who was expelled from every school he ever attended. He spent his time terrorising the local population, even running a protection racket whereby he and his adolescent enforcers demanded money from local merchants and shopkeepers as the price for not vandalising or burning down their premises. Most paid up and Clive was making a tidy packet, but as far as his family were concerned he was an embarrassment. With no prospect of him mending his ways, his relatives used their connections to secure him employment with the East India Company. They told him that in India he could make his fortune, but in truth they just wanted rid of him. In 1744, aged eighteen and somewhat reluctantly, Clive set sail for the Indian sub-continent.

The life expectancy of Europeans exiled to India was not high, with more than a third dying within three years of their arrival in the country, and the young Robert Clive soon came to understand why. His was a life of drudgery. He worked long hours in extreme heat for very low pay while the tedium of the work itself drove him to distraction. He was not considered a good worker and was in frequent trouble with his employers. He was also a manic depressive who soon took to opium as an escape from the grim reality of his life, an addiction which he never truly shed. Bored beyond all measure and in a dark place from which there appeared no escape, he resolved to kill himself. He put a gun to his head and pulled the trigger, but it failed to go off. He repeated the exercise but the same happened again. He later said that he took this to be a sign from God that he was being saved for something special. So he continued in his post, lazy, bored, and irascible; dreaming of riches and of how to make them. But it was events far away in Europe that were to determine Robert Clive's future. The ongoing rivalry between Britain and France was carried overseas to India and an opportunity presented itself for those audacious enough to take it. Robert Clive was nothing if not audacious.

On 4 September 1746, the city of Madras was attacked by the French and speedily overrun. Clive, along with many others, was taken prisoner, but during the lull between the city's surrender and the French occupation he organised an escape for himself and his colleagues to the safety of nearby Fort St David. The courage he displayed did not go unnoticed, and he was granted a commission in the East India Company's Army as a result. However, much to his disappointment, following the restoration of peace in 1748, he was returned to the tedium of his office, and a period of sustained depression soon followed. But Clive's willingness to seize the initiative and chance his arm had not been forgotten. He was soon to make his mark once again, this time at the 1751 Siege of Arcot.

Despite Britain and France being officially at peace, they continued to wage war by proxy abroad, particularly in India where Chanda Shahib, an ally of the French, had laid siege to the city of Arcot. Clive, in an act of both bravado and shameless self-promotion, declared that provided with the means to do so he would raise the siege. After consideration of the events at Madras the East India Company agreed, though they could not provide him with very much. His army would consist of just 200 European troops, 300 Indian sepoys, and three cannon.

Clive bided his time, eventually capturing the fort at Arcot under cover of a thunderstorm. He was then himself besieged for fifty days before a relief force of 2,000 Maratha Cavalry, under the command of Madina Ali Khan, an ally of the British, lifted the siege. Clive's capture of Arcot and his successful defence of it ended the campaign in the Carnatic region of India, securing a favourable peace for Britain while also increasing her possessions in the south of the country.

Robert Clive returned to Britain in 1753 a national hero and was even praised in the House of Commons by the then prime minister as a *'Heaven-sent General.'* But he was not to remain in Britain for long. Still ambitious, he knew there was more glory to be had and riches still to be made on

Robert Clive, 1st Baron Clive, Nathaniel Dance. (National Portrait Gallery)

the Indian sub-continent, so in 1755 he journeyed to India once more, no longer a lowly clerk but as the deputy governor of Fort St David. His return also happened to coincide with the accession of Siraj-ad-Daulah as the new Nawab of Bengal, a man with a barely disguised contempt for the British who was determined to assert control over his own territory. On 20 June 1755, he attacked and seized the British-held city of Calcutta.

By the time of Calcutta's fall most of the European inhabitants had already fled, but those who remained, some 146 souls, were rounded up and imprisoned in a tiny cell just fourteen feet by eighteen feet with one small window for air. According to one of those imprisoned, the surgeon John Zepheniah Holwell:

> By nine o'clock several had died, and many more were delirious. A frantic cry for water now became general, and one of the guards, more compassionate than his fellows, caused some to be brought to the bars, but in their impatience to receive it nearly all was spilt, and the little drank only seemed to increase their thirst. Self-control was soon lost, those in the remote parts of the room struggled to reach the window, and a fearful tumult ensued, in which the weakest were trampled or pressed to death. They raved, fought, prayed, blasphemed, and many fell exhausted to the floor, where suffocation brought an end to their torments.

Conditions were indeed appalling, and in the intense heat, crammed together and barely able to move, many were suffocated, died from exhaustion, or were trampled to death. By the time Siraj-ad-Daulah ordered the release of the prisoners the following morning 123 of them were already dead.

We have only Zepheniah Holwell's account of what really happened, but even taking into consideration a tendency for exaggeration the so-called *'Black Hole of Calcutta'* was either cruel negligence or a brutal act of murder.

An outraged Britain cried out for vengeance and Robert Clive was just the man to provide it. By now his reputation went before him and so he was put in command of operations to recapture Calcutta. Again, his army was small, just 2,000 troops, but this time he was supported by a naval squadron commanded by Admiral Charles Watson.

Clive wasted little time in taking the fight to the Nawab's much stronger army and his aggressive tactics worked, forcing the Nawab to abandon Calcutta on 5 February 1757.

Siraj-ad-Daulah remained unperturbed by this defeat, and was determined to renew hostilities with the British, this time with French support. Clive had not been idle, however, and unknown to the Nawab had been in negotiations with the commander of his army, Mir Jafar, who was opposed to his alliance with the French.

Mir Jafar was extremely ambitious, something that Clive was quick to exploit, and he agreed to consent to him replacing Siraj-Ad-Daulah as Nawab of Bengal in return for his support in any ensuing conflict. Mir Jafar would also make substantial payments totalling hundreds of thousands of pounds to the East India Company, its officials, its army, and to Clive himself. This treaty, which was kept secret both before and after it was signed, has since been used against Clive, condemned as he later was for his greed and duplicity.

Aware that long and tiresome negotiations between the East India Company and Siraj-ad-Daulah had achieved little, and that a renewal of hostilities was imminent, Clive took the initiative. He advanced his army (the Europeans in boats down the River Hooghly, his Indian sepoys made to walk) to confront the army of the Nawab. He established his headquarters in a hunting lodge in the mango groves of Plassey and awaited the Nawab's response.

As usual Clive's forces were slight: 1,100 European troops supported by 2,100 Indian sepoys and nine cannon. Siraj-ad-Daulah's army was enormous by comparison, and he could put in the field 50,000 infantry, 18,000 cavalry, war elephants and fifty-three cannon manned by French gunners.

Seeing the forces arrayed against him, Clive, perhaps for the first time in his life, demurred: to attack such an overwhelming force would be madness. That night he held a council of war, telling his senior officers that they were to decide: '*Whether in our present position without assistance it would be prudent to attack the Nawab or whether we should wait to be joined by some other power?*'

After a long and often heated debate, a vote was taken with the result of the ballot nine to seven against an immediate attack. Clive sided with those who counselled caution, a decision for which he was berated at length by Admiral Eyre Coote, who accused him of losing his nerve.

Alone that night Clive had a change of heart. He was later to say that the decision to fight came to him in a dream, but it seems he was more likely concerned for his reputation as a man of courage, or that he merely chose to trust in Mir Jafar. Either way, as the sun rose on the morning of 23 June

1757, Clive ordered his army to advance and confront the superior forces of Siraj-ad-Daulah.

It was swelteringly hot, and an almost impenetrable haze hung over the battlefield as both sides manoeuvred and exchanged preliminary artillery salvoes, but there was very little actual fighting. Neither side was willing to fully engage until late in the day Mir Jafar led his forces from the field. Witnessing this the remainder of the Nawab's army simply melted away.

Robert Clive had won one of the most decisive battles in world history for the loss of just twenty-two sepoys killed and fifty wounded. The Miracle of Plassey marked the beginning of British control of the Indian sub-continent and the creation of the Raj, the jewel in the crown of the British Empire, though there would be much hard fighting still to be done.

Already Governor of Bengal, Clive was now able not only to consolidate British rule (in the guise of the East India Company), but advance beyond it. However, at the age of just thirty-five his health was already failing him, and repeated bouts of depression were taking their toll. This did not prevent him from accumulating great personal wealth, and by the time he returned to England in 1760 his personal fortune was estimated to be £500,000.

In London he was greeted as an all-conquering man of genius, the hero of the empire, who subdued continents. The accolades and honours were countless: he was praised in parliament, received at court, and ennobled as Baron Clive of Plassey. But in his absence from India the efficient administration he had left behind became mired in sleaze and corruption, and so in April 1765 he once again set sail for the sub-continent.

The first thing Clive learned upon his arrival three months later was that Mir Jafar, who after Plassey had paid an assassin to murder Siraj-ad-Daulah before replacing him as Nawab of Bengal, had died, leaving him jewels to the value of £70,000 in his will. After receiving and pocketing the bequest Clive passed a law banning the acceptance of gifts by civil servants from native Indians. Yet despite this, and efforts to root out corruption in the army, reduce levels of taxation imposed on the peasantry, and stamp out smuggling, his attempts to clean up the administration were largely unsuccessful. By the time he left India for the last time in February 1767, very little had changed for the better.

Clive had only been away for two years, but he his reception in England was very different this time. The praise previously lavished upon him had not merely vanished, but had turned to criticism. His fame, great wealth and inflated status had induced feelings of envy and mistrust in many of the upper class, who were unwilling to accept that a man of so little background should fly so high. The qualities required for so great an elevation simply could not exist in a man of such common stock.

From 1772 onwards Clive was forced to defend himself against accusations of venality from both political enemies and previous friends. He was pilloried in the press for his greed and for taking bribes, placed under investigation, and made to justify his behaviour in the House of Lords. When questioned in Parliament about the vast personal fortune he had amassed in India he replied: '*By God, I am astonished at my own moderation.*'

Despite being cleared of all charges, the damage to Clive's reputation was permanent. The constant hounding from those he had previously considered friends, and their jealously, snobbery and lack of gratitude, took their toll on the always emotionally fragile Clive. Depressed and suffering from acute abdominal pains, he was found dead in his home on 22 November 1774. He had, it seemed, used a penknife to slit his own throat.

# Chapter 2

# Nelson and Trafalgar

By May 1803, the Peace of Amiens that had seen a brief lull after almost ten years of war between Britain and France was over. The renewal of hostilities was the result of Napoleon Bonaparte's determination to minimise British influence in Europe, impede its ability to trade abroad, and threaten its empire. Britain's response was to put in place a blockade of French ports and seize any ships bound for them. Bonaparte now demanded that Europe cease trading with Britain, and many countries had little choice but to comply.

Although Britain was in no position to fight a land war on the Continent, it remained determined to resist French hegemony in Europe and aimed to use its great wealth and abundance of resources to do so instead. Prime Minister William Pitt would finance the formation of the Third Coalition of Austria and Russia in opposition to Bonaparte. It was not the first time that 'Pitt's gold' had been used to thwart French ambitions, but Napoleon was determined that it should be the last. He gathered his *Grand Armée* at Boulogne for a planned invasion of England to end once and for all the meddling of this arrogant 'nation of shopkeepers'.

Britain was ready for war but ill-prepared for battle: its army remained relatively small, and it had no outstanding general to call upon. Despite coastal fortifications being strengthened the militia system upon which their defence fell was little more than a refuge for vagabonds, thieves, and banditti. Few doubted that if Napoleon landed his *Grand Armée* on the shores of England it would triumph quickly, but then Britain's military strength did not lie with its army but with its navy, and one man in particular: Admiral Lord Viscount Nelson.

Nelson was a controversial figure, whose judgement had been called into question: if not when on active service, then at least in the arrangement of his domestic affairs.

Horatio Nelson was born on 29 September 1758, in the village of Burnham Thorpe, Norfolk, the sixth of eleven children. His father Edmund was a clergyman and although the family were of modest means, they were well connected through Nelson's mother, Catherine Suckling, who was the niece of Robert Walpole, Britain's first *de facto* prime minister and the richest man in the country. These connections were to serve Nelson well throughout his career.

At the age of twelve the young Horatio enlisted in the Royal Navy as an ordinary able seaman, but his uncle, who commanded the ship, soon promoted him to midshipman.

Personally courageous, and a fine seaman who understood naval tactics and strategy, Nelson's rise through the ranks was nothing short of meteoric. By the age of twenty he was already commanding his own vessel.

Nelson's battle scars told their own story. On 19 June 1794, during the successful siege of Calvi in Corsica, he was caught in a shell burst that splintered his right eye. When told that he would in time lose the use of it he remarked that it was a mere inconvenience, for he had another. It was typical Nelson.

Respected by his peers within the navy, if not always by the Admiralty, Nelson first came to national prominence on 14 February 1797, when

Viscount Admiral Horatio Nelson, Lemuel Francis Abbott (1797). (National Maritime Museum)

the British and Spanish fleets clashed off Cape St Vincent. Fearing that his commanding officer, Sir John Jervis, was about to let the enemy escape, Nelson disobeyed orders to break away and attack three ships of the Spanish vanguard. He appeared to have over-reached himself, as in the vicious exchange of broadsides the out-gunned British were clearly coming off worse. But Nelson wasn't a man willing to accept failure and, drawing his sword, he rallied his men and led a boarding party onto the opposing *San Nicolas* with such ferocity that he not only swept the defenders aside but went on to board the *San Josef*, which had pulled alongside to assist.

Viewing events from afar, Sir John Jervis was less belligerent and, much to Nelson's chagrin, the Spanish fleet, though defeated, was allowed to withdraw relatively intact. Jervis was to publicly rebuke Nelson for disobeying orders, but privately acknowledged that it was his actions that had secured victory, though he omitted this from his official report. Nelson, not willing to be overlooked in such a manner, had his own account of the battle published in *The Times* newspaper.

Following the Battle of Cape St Vincent, Nelson was given command of his own squadron and ordered to lie off Cadiz and intercept Spanish treasure ships arriving from South America. This he did successfully but it was dull work, and, in the meantime, he had convinced the Admiralty in London to support his plan to capture the port of Santa Cruz de Tenerife.

This was not a success. The Spanish defences were to prove more formidable than at first thought, with several boats shot to pieces before they could land and those Marines who made it ashore dispersed over a wide area. Nelson tried to bring order to chaos by leading from the front as he always did, but was struck down by a musket ball which shattered the bone in his right arm.

As the attack stalled Nelson's officers formed a protective ring around him, but the surgeon who was in attendance could do little to treat the wound and had no choice but to amputate the arm.

Nelson returned to England to nurse his wounds in great pain and no little despair, as he believed the fiasco at Santa Cruz de Tenerife and his disability guaranteed the end of his naval career. However, the heroic way in which he had fallen had enhanced rather than damaged his reputation. Even so, a long period of rehabilitation and the war continuing at sea without him proved a great frustration.

In early 1798, the British became aware that Bonaparte was gathering a large army and many ships in and around the area of Toulon on the

Mediterranean coast. It was evident that he was planning a campaign, but where exactly remained unknown.

In fact Napoleon intended the conquest of Egypt, a long-cherished dream of the French, who considered it the cradle of civilisation. Sentiment aside, Napoleon also perceived its strategic value as a place from which he could threaten Britain's interests in India.

The French fleet sailed from Toulon on 17 May, bound for Egypt, stopping off on the way to seize the island of Malta for France. Nelson, who had since resumed active service, was given command of a squadron and despatched from the main fleet, still stationed off Cadiz, to find the French fleet, track its course, and intercept it if possible.

More than once Nelson almost stumbled across the French invasion force, but it wasn't until 28 July that he at last received intelligence that its destination was Alexandria in Egypt.

In the meantime, Napoleon had disembarked his troops in haste, aware that the British fleet was likely nearby.

Nelson arrived not long after only to find the French fleet gone. It had moved further up the coast to Aboukir Bay at the mouth of the River Nile, where the French admiral François-Paul Brueys had moored it in battle formation.

Although Aboukir Bay provided little obvious protection, its waters were shallow and it was thought they would impede Nelson's manoeuvrability, thereby preventing him from launching a sustained attack, and that even if he did try to do so Brueys had moored his ships close enough to the shore to force him into what could only be a frontal assault.

However, the shoals of Aboukir Bay were not as shallow as Brueys had imagined and moreover there was more than enough room for Nelson to get between the shore and the French battle line. And it was an opportunity he was quick to exploit, isolating the French vanguard and squeezing it from both sides. Caught in a vice-like grip it was raked with a fire so ferocious that it was utterly destroyed. Now outgunned and unable to manoeuvre, Brueys had no choice but to stand and fight. It was to be a one-sided affair.

Even so, the French fought hard and as a result sustained heavy casualties, including Admiral Brueys, who, shot through and dismembered by a cannon ball, nonetheless remained at his post until he bled to death.

At 22.00 the French flagship *Orient*, which had been ablaze for some time, detonated in a massive explosion that not only tore it apart, but also severely damaged several other ships nearby, killing more than a thousand men.

This was in effect a *coup de grace* and although some French ships resumed the fight on the morrow the outcome was no longer in doubt. By the time the fighting ceased thirteen French ships had been destroyed or captured with 5,000 men killed and wounded. The destruction would have been complete had not Admiral Pierre-Charles de Villeneuve, with four ships, escaped the carnage under the cover of darkness.

For the loss of no ships and just 267 men killed Lord Nelson had shattered Napoleon's dreams of a Middle East empire, even if he was to remain in Egypt for a further two years, plundering it of its treasures and heritage.

When Britain learned of Nelson's victory at the Battle of the Nile the nation erupted in an orgy of celebration as people thronged the streets, bonfires were lit, and fireworks blazed across the night sky.

Nelson was praised in an address to Parliament by King George III, awarded a pension of £2,000 a year in perpetuity, and received a baronetcy; he later became a viscount.

Following his triumph Nelson sailed to Naples where he was received as a hero. The wife of the ambassador to the kingdom of Naples, Lady Emma Hamilton, breathlessly received him with the words, '*Oh God, is it possible!*' before promptly fainting. If this was not exactly love at first sight, it was certainly a step on the way to seduction.

Emma Hamilton,
George Romney (1784).
(Rothschild Collections)

Amy Lyon, the daughter of a blacksmith, who became a dancer, artist's model and society whore, had risen high, but it had been a hard road of failed affairs, abandonment, and little dignity. She had for a time been the lover of Sir Henry Featherstonehaugh, but the relationship came to an end when, concerned about her continued fecundity following an unwanted pregnancy, he passed her onto Sir Charles Greville, who had long expressed an interest.

Sir Charles took Amy in on condition that she changed her name to the more respectable Emma, and remained out of sight unless called upon to entertain his guests. The relationship was only a year old when, under pressure to make a good and profitable marriage, Emma became an inconvenience to him. Unwilling to do ill by her he persuaded his uncle Lord William Hamilton to take her off his hands.

This was hardly a love match, as Hamilton was more than twice Emma's age. He only reluctantly and for the good of the family acquiesced to his nephew's request. Emma, weary of being passed around on sale or return, eventually persuaded Hamilton not just to keep her as a mistress, but to marry her. As Lady Hamilton she did nothing to disguise her admiration for the hero Nelson and they soon became lovers.

As if the very public cuckolding of a high-ranking British official (though it was seemingly done with Hamilton's approval) wasn't bad enough, Nelson was also married. He had wed Frances Nisbet, a Caribbean plantation owner's daughter, twelve years earlier.

Happy enough at first, the marriage soon began to sour in large part due to Frances's inability to conceive, but she remained devoted to her husband, tending to his wounds, both physical and emotional, whenever he returned from sea, and caring for his elderly father, but her devotion made her neither interesting nor exciting. Lady Emma was both. Increasingly estranged from his wife, Nelson still wrote letters to her that were fulsome in their praise of the beautiful and exotic Lady Emma. Frances's letters to him would later remain unopened.

Nelson's behaviour scandalised respectable society and the rewards that his achievements might have merited ceased, as, shunned at high table and already under scrutiny for his cavalier attitude towards orders, his judgement now came into question. He was, it was said, no gentleman.

As Nelson flaunted his relationship with Lady Emma, often with Lord Hamilton close behind, he accumulated opprobrium, but it was only a matter of time before the next crisis would emerge and his services would be called upon once more.

An alliance of Russia, Prussia, Sweden and Denmark, known as the League of Neutrality, had been formed to oppose Britain's continuing blockade of European ports. Such an alliance could not be permitted to stand and, with negotiations making little progress, the decision was made to destroy the combined Danish and Norwegian fleet stationed at Copenhagen. The British would have to act swiftly, however, before the seas thawed sufficiently to release the Russian fleet from its ice-bound sojourn on the Baltic coast.

Despite being acknowledged as the outstanding naval commander of his day, doubts persisted about Nelson's character and he was once more denied overall command. This went to Admiral Sir Hyde Parker, a cautious man, who, worried by the size of the fleet that opposed him and wary of the fortress guns that protected it, dithered about committing to an all-out assault. Nelson, on the other hand, was eager to get the fighting underway, believing that any delay only played into the hands of the enemy.

At 10.00 on 2 April 1801, Nelson moved his ships into position to attack the weaker end of the Danish line, intending to rake and board them one at a time, making room for marines to land and storm the fortress of Tre Kroner. Hyde Parker believed it would be a hard slog and so it turned out.

By midday little progress had been made and, peering into the fog that partially shrouded the action from his view, Hyde Parker could see three British ships of the line clearly in distress. He signalled to Nelson to cease the attack and withdraw.

However, by this time superior British gunnery was taking effect, and, though the fortress was not taken, its guns had been effectively silenced and the left of the Danish line was beginning to crumble. Aware of this Nelson put a telescope to his blind eye and remarked to a subordinate, '*I really do not see the signal.*'

The attack continued and by late afternoon it was clear the Danes were losing, but they still possessed a powerful reserve and the British were exhausted. It would in the end take a combination of bluff and threat from Nelson to secure victory, demonstrating that he could talk a good fight as well as engaging in one.

This was yet another triumph for Lord Nelson and no one could be in any doubt that the victory had been his and his alone. He had, it was said, the 'Nelson touch'. At last, he received the promotion he had always wanted and became Admiral of the Fleet.

Admiral Lord Viscount Nelson possessed that rare quality in a military commander: he was both loved and respected by his men. He not only brought them victory in battle, but shared their dangers and had the scars to prove it. He was also a humane commander by the standards of the day, disavowing the more brutal punishments and relying on his personal authority to maintain discipline.

On 2 December 1804, at a grand ceremony held at Notre Dame Cathedral in Paris, Napoleon Bonaparte, who had been the effective sole ruler of France since 1799, crowned himself Emperor. That he did so with the Pope present was indicative of his impatience to get the job done. He was no less impatient to eradicate Britain as a threat to his hegemony in Europe and French interests around the world.

As Napoleon gathered his army at Boulogne, he imagined a swift victory, but this would require control of the English Channel, if only for a few days. However, the powerful Royal Navy stood in his way, as did its formidable Commander-in-Chief.

Responsibility for neutralising the British fleet would fall to Admiral Pierre-Charles de Villeneuve, who had barely escaped the catastrophe at Aboukir Bay eight years earlier. A very different man to Nelson in both character and temperament, he had been born into an aristocratic family that had survived the ravages of the Revolution and was a career naval officer whose guiding light was honour, something he had been born to, not a meritorious badge of recognition earned in battle. He did not feel the need to seek glory. But he did have a plan.

Nelson, contrary to received wisdom, did not maintain a close blockade of the French ports, but hoped instead to entice their fleet into open sea where they could be forced to give battle. Villeneuve intended to seize this opportunity to evade the British fleet and sail west to attack British possessions in the Caribbean, thereby luring Nelson away from the Channel in hot pursuit. He would then turn back, link up with the Spanish fleet, and disperse those British ships still on station, allowing the French invasion barges to cross the Channel unimpeded. It was a good plan, and when Villeneuve sailed from Toulon in March 1805, easily evading the British blockade, Nelson, misreading his intentions, at first sailed for the Mediterranean on a wild goose chase before realising his mistake. Unfavourable winds then delayed him further until he was more than a month's travelling distance behind.

But now Villeneuve dithered, and he remained in the Caribbean for three months doing very little. It wasn't until news reached him that Nelson's fleet had been sighted off Antigua that he embarked upon the return journey: the valuable time won had been squandered.

On 22 July Villeneuve encountered a small British force off Cape Finisterre and in a brisk firefight two Spanish vessels were lost. This seemed to shake Villeneuve's confidence, and instead of continuing the engagement, which should have been a one-sided affair, he broke it off and returned to Cadiz in defiance of demands from his subordinates that he not do so. Before long he was blockaded in port once more.

Losing patience with his admiral on 26 August, Napoleon broke camp at Boulogne and marched his army into Germany to counter the threat posed by the formation of the Third Coalition. For the time being at least Britain was freed from the threat of possible invasion.

In September Villeneuve was ordered to break out from Cadiz and sail for the Mediterranean, but he chose to ignore the order. This proved the final straw for Napoleon, who now sought to replace the admiral, writing that: *'Villeneuve does not have the strength of character to command a frigate. He lacks determination and has no moral courage.'*

It was only now, with his honour impugned, that Villeneuve decided to act, but he did so with trepidation. Nelson would fight, and he was likely to adopt unorthodox methods. How could he anticipate the unexpected?

Previous experience had taught Villeneuve that Nelson would likely seek to close and board as soon as possible and so, to counter this threat, he had recruited some 4,000 mostly Tyrolean sharpshooters to remain high in the rigging and rake the decks of the British ships in any close-quarter combat. He also thought that Nelson's fleet was more powerful than his own, although he was mistaken: The combined French and Spanish fleet under Villeneuve's command consisted of forty-one vessels including thirty-three ships of the line, carrying 2,652 guns and 25,200 men. The British fleet under Nelson had thirty-three vessels including twenty-seven ships of the line, with 2,178 guns and 17, 076 men.

On 18 October, the Franco-Spanish fleet sailed from Cadiz harbour, but three days later, informed that Nelson was approaching, Villeneuve once more had a loss of nerve and ordered the fleet's return to port. However, light winds prevented progress: he had left it too late.

It was standard practice in naval warfare of the time for opposing fleets to form up in line of battle parallel to one another and then exchange broadsides at close range, which allowed for easier communication, greater control, and increased manoeuvrability, but it also ensured that few battles were fought to a conclusion. Such an outcome was simply intolerable to Nelson who was intent on the utter destruction of the enemy. Nothing less would do.

On consecutive nights Nelson dined with his captains and outlined his plan for the forthcoming battle. He would drive straight at the enemy line in two columns, piercing it twice, thus dividing it into three separate parts and causing chaos as a result. The enemy ships would then be engaged as quickly as possible, creating a mêlée so ferocious and confused that they would have no time to recover.

Speed was of the essence, with no time being given for the separate parts of the enemy fleet to manoeuvre in support of one another, and no opportunity given for them to decline battle.

Nelson had complete faith in the superiority of British gunnery, seamanship and valour, and was in no doubt that in any fight they would prevail. Morale among the crews was also high, with each man from captain to cabin boy knowing his job and the role he had to play.

Such self-assuredness had not been much in evidence in the weeks of shore leave prior to Nelson's re-joining the fleet, when his mood could best have been described as melancholic.

Nelson had stayed at the home of the Hamiltons, who were still living together as man and wife, where he spent precious time with Horatia, his infant daughter by Emma. Although the young Horatia was aware who her father was, her mother's identity was kept from her for many years, with Emma claiming to be her guardian.

Regardless of the gossip and the rumours that surrounded their relationship, these were idyllic times for Horatio and Emma. Even so, a certain fatalism had come to dominate Nelson's character: he was uncharacteristically affectionate towards friends and colleagues, spoke often in the past tense and even at one point visited a leading London undertaker to purchase a coffin.

Despite the contentment he found in the company of Emma and his daughter, he remained eager to return to the fleet and get the job done.

Things were very different for Pierre-Charles de Villeneuve, who was both under pressure to act and knowing both the ability of his opponent and the state of the navy he commanded, fearful of failure.

Unlike the Royal Navy, which was essential to Britain's continued dominance of world trade, the French fleet was not the source of Napoleon Bonaparte's power, but merely the means to an end. As such, many of the crews were inexperienced and poorly trained, with promotion by aristocratic privilege attained by right and not on merit. Similarly, the condition of the Spanish fleet under the command of Admiral Frederico Gravina reflected a power that had been in decline for many years.

Nelson left nothing to chance and he confidently predicted victory, declaring that at least twenty ships would be taken. But still that sense of fatalism remained. As a final meeting with his subordinates broke up, he said to the captain of the *Euryalus*: '*God bless you Blackwood, I shall never see you again.*'

Having been dissuaded from wearing his full-dress uniform, Nelson donned his second-best uniform, but having adorned it with awards, badges and gold braid he remained a conspicuous and obvious target.

As dawn broke on 21 October 1805, the drums rolled and the men prepared for battle: the big 24-pounder guns were rolled into place, portals opened and the ammunition, large iron cannon balls, grapeshot, and ball and chain, designed to tear up and bring down rigging, was stockpiled. The cooking fires were doused, the decks were laid with sand and moveable items were lashed down as men took up positions with sweat on the their brows, lumps in their throats and mouths dry with nervous anticipation.

As the two fleets closed the anxiety was palpable. At 11.45 Nelson raised his famous signal: '*England expects that every man will do his duty.*'

Villeneuve's line, which stretched for more than five miles, appeared ragged and poorly organised, playing into Nelson's hands, but he also knew the risks he was running by approaching in column, which left his ships vulnerable to the broadsides of the enemy without being able to respond in kind. Also, the numerical superiority of the Franco-Spanish fleet might leave individual British ships isolated and subjected to the sustained fire of two or even three enemy vessels.

Nelson, aboard the *Victory,* led the Windward Squadron on a course directly for Villeneuve's flagship, the *Bucentaure*. Captain Eliab Harvey, aboard the *Temeraire,* fearing that the admiral would expose himself to unnecessary danger, tried to provide protection by getting ahead of the *Victory* until ordered back into line.

Finding his way to the *Bucentaure* blocked by the *Redoubtable*, Nelson ordered it rammed and, supported by the *Temeraire*, opened a ferocious barrage at point-blank range on both ships and a little later the approaching *Santissima Trinidad.*

The fighting was brutal as limbs were torn off by hurtling cannon balls, the decks were raked with musket fire, wood splinters flew everywhere, rigging collapsed, fires broke out trapping men below and many were thrown overboard and drowned. Indeed, so lethal was the bombardment that some of the French, who had not seen action before, refused to open

Battle of Trafalgar, William Clarkson Stanfield (1836). (Public domain via Wikimedia Commons)

their gun ports and return fire, with many deserting their posts. As they were soon to find out, there was nowhere to hide in the confines of a ship.

At the same time as Nelson was engaged in a life and death struggle, his second-in-command, Cuthbert Collingwood, leading the Leeward Squadron on his ship the *Royal Sovereign*, also smashed into the enemy line, firing a broadside of such ferocity upon the Spanish *Santa Anna* that it killed or maimed 400 men and disabled fourteen guns. Reduced to little more than a hulk the *Santa Anna* soon surrendered.

By this time both fleets were becoming fully engaged, and superior British gunnery and the inexperience of the enemy, who resisted fiercely in some places but not so much in others, was taking its toll as they were increasingly overwhelmed.

*Victory* was taking fearful punishment from the combined guns of three enemy ships. Its wheel had been shot away, broken masts and torn rigging littered the deck, a squadron of marines lay dead and dying, their bodies ripped apart by a cascading cannon ball, and Nelson's personal aide was killed, as was his replacement. Captain Hardy had barely escaped with his life on several occasions. Nelson reassured him, '*this is too warm work to last long'*.

For all the bloody chaos aboard the *Victory* the French *Redoubtable* was faring worse and, with its gun decks destroyed in a desperate attempt to turn the tide, its captain ordered that the *Victory* be boarded.

The French fought with great determination and some initial success, but the *Temeraire*, coming alongside, raked the deck with grapeshot causing great loss of life and repelling the invaders.

Throughout the fighting Nelson had been a very visible presence, encouraging his men and showing no fear as he strolled calmly along the quarter-deck in the company of Captain Hardy. But at 1.27pm, just as the battle was reaching its climax, he was shot by a sharpshooter atop the mizzenmast of the *Redoubtable*. The musket ball penetrated his left shoulder, pierced his lung, and broke his spine.

As he lay upon the deck in great pain, surrounded by anxious staff, he muttered: '*They have done for me Hardy, my back is shot through.*' Nelson knew he was dying and told the ship's surgeon, William Beatty, '*there is nothing you can do for me*'.

Pausing for a moment to advise a young midshipman on how best to use the tiller, Nelson was taken below decks to the cockpit where he was laid out with others who had had been wounded in the service of their country, in a scene the ship's chaplain, Alexander Scott, described as 'a butcher's

Death of Nelson (1805), ArthurWilliam Devis. (Public domain via Wikimedia Commons)

yard'. It was certainly no place of peace to end a life cut short at the very moment of its greatest glory.

Less than an hour after Nelson was shot the *Redoubtable* and *Santissima Trinidad* succumbed, followed shortly by Villeneuve on the *Bucentaure*, who was taken into captivity. The sight of the *Bucentaure* raising the white flag had a devastating effect on French morale.

The vanguard of the Franco-Spanish fleet, which had initially sailed away from the fighting until being ordered back by Villeneuve, now fired an indiscriminate broadside before sailing away once more. Others tried to disengage and make their escape but with little success.

Sporadic fighting continued but the outcome of the battle was no longer in doubt and as the enemy ships surrendered one after another it became increasingly evident that the victory was total. For the loss of no ships, 458 men killed and 1,208 wounded the powerful Franco-Spanish fleet had been destroyed and the threat to British liberty eradicated. Combined, the French and Spanish had lost twenty-two ships sunk or captured, with many of those that escaped damaged beyond repair, and 3,053 men killed, 2,438 wounded, and a further 8,000 taken prisoner.

However, the nightmare was not over for those who had been fortunate enough to escape the carnage, as a violent storm blew up and many of the burned and crippled hulks sank, drowning more than 3,000 prisoners locked below decks. The British had to abandon all but four of their prizes.

Throughout this time, Nelson, having been informed of events, had continued to issue instructions until he was too weak to do so. When he was told by Hardy of the scale of the victory he breathed a sigh of relief and remarked: '*Thank God, I have done my duty.*'

At 4.30pm Nelson died. His last recorded words were '*God and country*'. His body was placed in a casket of brandy, which was then lashed to the mainmast and placed under armed guard.

The victory at Trafalgar was greeted with relief and joy, though the celebratory spirit was dampened somewhat by the news of Nelson's death.

Some suggested that it had been too high a price to pay, but is any price too great for the life of a nation? When Emma Hamilton was told of her beloved Horatio's death, she was quite literally shocked into silence, later writing that she was unable to speak, utter a sound, or even shed a tear for many hours.

Nelson was accorded the honour of a state funeral, in a display of national mourning never seen before and only rarely since. On 8 January

1806, following five days of public mourning, Nelson's body was taken from its resting place at Greenwich Hospital and placed in a royal barge, draped in black velvet and decorated with ostrich feathers, which was accompanied by numerous vessels of all kinds down the River Thames to Westminster. Thousands viewed the procession from the riverbank and bridges.

The body was taken to the Admiralty Building, where it remained overnight. The funeral cortège continued to St Paul's Cathedral the following day as the entire city turned out to watch.

The coffin, which had been placed on a carriage designed to resemble the *Victory* and adorned with battle trophies, had both a military escort and so many principal mourners that the procession took hours to make the short journey to St Paul's.

But for all the ceremonial fanfare and expressions of deep sorrow, the scandal of Nelson's domestic affairs had barely diminished and so there was no formal royal representation at the funeral. Indeed, when the Prince of Wales requested permission to attend, he was informed that he could only do so in a private capacity.

Similarly, Emma Hamilton was refused permission to attend the funeral. Her status as an adulteress was deemed morally repugnant and a stain on the reputation of the deceased.

The interior of St Paul's Cathedral was decorated with reminders of Nelson's career: his trophies, uniforms and awards, with captured French and Spanish battle flags hanging from the rafters.

The ceremony lasted four hours and long into the night before the coffin was placed in a marble tomb that had once been intended for Cardinal Wolsey and finally lowered into the crypt of the cathedral. The final words were spoken: '*The hero, who in the moment of victory, fell covered with immortal glory.*'

The glory, it seemed, did not extend to Emma Hamilton, the woman he loved. She had refused to countenance divorcing her husband while he still lived, but since his death she had been excitedly contemplating her marriage to Nelson. But it wasn't to be.

Ignored by the Government despite Nelson's request in his will that they '*take care to maintain her rank in life*', Emma, always generous to a fault, quickly squandered the inheritance left to her by Sir William and, by trying to maintain a status for herself and her daughter that she believed Nelson would be proud of, she was soon heavily in debt. Still, she continued to petition the Government for support, but the publication of letters between her and Nelson outlining the details of their affair only created further scandal. By the summer of 1812 she was in prison for debt.

Fearing that further creditors lurked in the shadows, upon her release she fled with her daughter to France. Impoverished, weak through illness, and abandoned by her friends, she turned to drink as her only solace, dying in Calais on 15 January 1815, aged 49. Following her mother's death Horatia returned to England in secret to live with her aunt.

Ignoring her father's wish that she should forever be known as Nelson, Horatia married the Reverend Philip Ward and lived a quiet life in Norfolk as the mother of eight children, refusing all opportunities to benefit from her famous parentage. She died on 6 March 1881, aged 80.

Napoleon Bonaparte did nothing to facilitate the release of Admiral de Villeneuve (who had been permitted to attend Nelson's funeral) despite his frequent requests for him to do so. In the end, he was forced to make his own way back to France, where Napoleon refused to receive him or answer his letters. On 22 April 1806 he was found dead in his hotel room having been stabbed multiple times. The verdict was suicide.

In recognition of Admiral Lord Viscount Nelson's achievements, in 1843 the 170ft Nelson's Column was unveiled in Trafalgar Square, London, where it has since dominated the city's skyline. It is Britain's greatest monument to Britain's greatest hero.

# PART NINE

# The Cultural Life

# Chapter 1

# Distractions

Georgian Britain witnessed a flourishing of the arts unprecedented in the nation's history. Decades of political turmoil and civil strife had long stifled artistic endeavour, but the new optimism that now prevailed saw a genius unleashed that was to impact every aspect of society.

Many of our favourite artists today were Georgians. J.M.W. Turner, for example, was born in 1775 during the reign of George III; while John Constable's famous 'Haywain' (he was born just a year after Turner) was painted during the Regency. Similarly popular were the portraits of Sir Thomas Lawrence and Thomas Gainsborough, whose idealised depictions of the feminine divine would set the standard of womanhood for decades to come.

Indeed, having one's portrait painted, which was both expensive and time-consuming, was considered a mark of one's status, though few paid as much money as the Marquess of Rockingham did to the great equine artist George Stubbs for a portrait of his favourite racehorse Whistlejacket.

This was also the time when the British countryside, its nooks and crannies, its lakes and mountains, its remoter places, were viewed with awe rather than dread and the desire to record it in all its natural beauty saw the emergence of the first great landscape artists. Not all artists focused on beauty, of course. William Hogarth used his eye as a mirror on society, and his brush as a critique of that society; while William Blake, who would later write the famous hymn 'Jerusalem', painted on a large canvas an ill-defined and abstract religiosity.

In 1768, the Royal Academy of Arts was established in London under its first president, Sir Joshua Reynolds. Open to all artists, it soon found an audience among those who possessed a cultural hinterland, and its annual summer exhibition would become so popular it became a feature on the social calendar.

In the literary sphere popular fiction became a reality for the first time, not just the bawdy tales of Tom Jones and Tristram Shandy, but the political satire of Jonathan Swift's *Gulliver's Travels* and the exploration of violence against and disregard for women described in Samuel Richardson's 1740 novel *Pamela*. New genres were also created with the Gothic novels of Horace Walpole and the enduring legacy of horror bequeathed us by Mary Shelley in her novel *Frankenstein*.

Jane Austen, whose books we most readily associate with the Georgian era, was never well read during her lifetime. The fact that, as a woman, she published anonymously, a trend that would continue well into the reign of Queen Victoria, no doubt restricted sales. Though it is also possible that her books, as brilliant as they are, had a subject matter and specificity of purpose that was always likely to be viewed more fondly with the passage of time.

We should remember at this point that despite the books mentioned above being, for the most part, best-sellers that ran into many editions, the overall readership remained small. With little formal education to speak of, most people remained barely able to read or write. So perhaps, as today, cultural pursuits remained minority pursuits.

The publication of *Lyrical Ballads,* a 1798 collaboration between William Wordsworth and Samuel Taylor Coleridge, made poetry in English popular for the first time. It was a transformative moment in English literary history, as poetry engaged with grubby politics and the realities of life. As Shelley famously remarked, *'poets and philosophers are the unacknowledged legislators of the world'*.

Britain was changing in other ways too. The imaginings and aspirations of the people were mirrored in physical changes. Parks designed and developed by men such as Lancelot 'Capability' Brown altered the landscape, while architects like Robert Adam and John Nash transformed Britain's towns and cities with their neo-classical designs.

An expanding middle class also provided a lucrative market for the exquisite creations of designers and entrepreneurs such as the furniture maker Thomas Chippendale and the potter Josiah Wedgewood, whose famous Jasperware, made at his Etruria works in Stoke-on-Trent, would become an essential feature of any mantlepiece in an aspirational home.

I have focused a great deal in this book on the harsher realities of life in Georgian Britain, but it was also a time of great refinement, perhaps the pinnacle of beauty and well-mannered gentility. That is the aspect of Georgian life we choose to remember and so admire today. It was not the life experienced by most at the time, but they shared in it too, in their way. The common folk may not have possessed or enjoyed beautiful *objets d'art*, but they made them with skilled hands in the factories and workshops. They may not have lived in beautiful buildings, but they saw them; they may not have owned the parks, but they could walk their pathways.

# Chapter 2

# Style

The Georgian era was a time of great splendour and display, when those of substance, and they were few, would promenade their finery for all to see. The cream of English society, the 1,500 or so families that could trace a noble lineage known as the 'Ton', and those of the *nouveau riche* raised in status and emboldened of spirit by overseas trade and the expansion of empire, were eager that others should know of their privilege and power, even on streets where the poverty in the air was absolute, pungent, and infected the very nostrils of those who breathed it.

The highlight of any year was the London Season, which ran from January to July, though the summer months could be curtailed should the plague be in town. Hyde Park was a popular destination for daily entertainments and barely disguised illicit trysts for rich and poor alike; but it was the rich, with their parasols and canes, on horseback and in gilded carriages who set the scene. Nowhere else in Europe could the rich so flagrantly flaunt their wealth without fear of riot and revolution, though they were not immune to robbery, and a gentleman rarely journeyed unarmed.

The place to be seen was Rotten Row: a gravel pathway lit by oil lamps at night that had been commissioned by William III to provide a safe route through Hyde Park, where many an unfortunate traveller had fallen victim to armed thieves and highwaymen. Created as the King's Road, its popular name was a corruption of the original French '*Route du Roi*'.

Having put themselves on display throughout the day, gentlemen who had no other priorities to impinge on their time would retire to attend early evening soirées where they would take tea and eat cake before departing to prepare for the night-time ball, a lavish affair where the women, resplendent in heels, silk stockings, powdered wigs and heavily brocaded dresses, flirted with men whose boots could never be too shiny nor their breeches too tight.

All this peacockery did have a purpose, however: it provided the opportunity for young ladies to meet eligible bachelors, future husbands with prospects and a title to inherit. It was known as the 'Marriage Mart.'

Lady Georgiana Cavendish, Duchess of Devonshire, Thomas Gainsborough. (Public domain via Wikimedia Commons)

The fashion icons of the day included Georgiana Cavendish, Duchess of Devonshire, who was famous for her high powdered and perfumed wigs, adorned with coloured ribbons and ostrich feathers – much copied by the ladies of the day. Her male equivalent was George Bryan 'Beau' Brummell, son of the Private Secretary to Prime Minister Lord North and close friend of the Prince Regent and future King George IV, a man never shy to neglect his royal duties in favour of his vanity.

The fate which had befallen the aristocracy in France during the revolution tempered English extravagance and excess for a time. Marie Antoinette's execution led the ladies of England to wear more modest and looser-fitting muslin dresses rather than the lace and silk of old, with their cleavages less prominent and hidden from sight. The gentleman too may have temporarily lost his swagger, but with the voices of dissent silenced at home, confidence was soon restored, and Beau Brummell led the way with his love of dark coats over brilliant white linen shirts sprinkled with glitter and sewn with jewels that sparkled beneath the chandeliers, elaborately knotted neckerchiefs and knee-length boots polished with champagne to within an inch of their lives. He was no less extravagant in his claims than he was in his dress. He would tell the story of how he resigned his commission in the Royal Hussars when they were assigned to Manchester, declaring that he could not bear to be in a place so lacking in style. He also claimed to spend five hours every day bathing, dressing, and preparing his hair.

Such was Beau Brummell's fame that the Prince Regent himself consulted England's foremost dandy on how to dress before appearing in public, but when, in July 1813, at a Masquerade Ball held in the prince's

Who's Your Fat Friend? illustration James Godwin, engraved by the Dalziel Brothers. (The Wits and Beauxs of Society)

honour, feeling he was being ignored, he spoke loudly and often of George's excessive weight, all that changed. The prince never forgave him.

An admiring public is always fickle and in any dispute between Brummell and the future king of England there could be only one winner. Deserted by friends and patrons alike, in 1816 Brummell fled penniless to France to avoid the debtors' prison. He remained well-connected enough to secure a job at the British Consulate in Caen, but he found provincialism dull and, incapable of either sobriety or meaningful endeavour, he soon found himself in a French debtors' prison. Those few friends still sympathetic to him paid for his release and begged him to return home to England but he refused, instead remaining in France where he died alone in an asylum on 30 March 1840, aged sixty-one, having been driven insane by syphilis.

Lady Georgiana, Duchess of Devonshire, had courted controversy all her life and not just because of her outrageous fashion sense. She'd also had a series of torrid and very public affairs, was outspoken in her views at a time when women were expected to be seen but not heard, was frequently intoxicated, and had an addiction to the card table and roulette wheel that by the time of her death aged just forty-eight in 1806, saw her leave gambling debts the equivalent today of over £3,000,000.

The Prince Regent became King George IV on 29 January 1820. He had long considered himself to be the most fashionable and handsome prince in Europe, but now, without Beau Brummell to guide him, he felt lost and sought constant validation. In the end, his increasingly absurd attempts to be admired made him a laughing stock. So much so, that when the most lampooned monarch in British history died on 26 June 1830, grossly overweight and barely able to stand, he was little mourned. His obituary *The Times* read:

> There never was an individual less regretted by his fellow creatures than this deceased King. What eye has wept for him? What heart has throbbed one heave of unmercenary sorrow? If he ever had a friend – a devoted friend in any rank of life – we protest that the name of him or her has ever reached us.

# Chapter 3

# The Duchess of Richmond's Ball

The Duchess of Richmond's Ball was always one of the most eagerly anticipated events on the social calendar, but this year was different. It was 15 June 1815, and since Napoleon Bonaparte's return to Paris from his enforced exile on the Mediterranean island of Elba almost three months earlier the armies of the Allied coalition formed to oppose him had been gathering. The vanguard was camped around Brussels near the border with France. The Duke of Richmond was responsible for the defence of Brussels in the event of a French attempt to seize the city, but his wife, Charlotte Lennox, remained determined that the ball should go ahead regardless. She approached the Duke of Wellington, commanding the Allied forces, for permission. He replied: '*Duchess, you may give your Ball without fear of interruption.*'

Despite the many foreign dignitaries in attendance, with the cream of the British nobility serving in the Duke of Wellington's army (including three of her own sons), the guest list had a familiar feel to it, and the house the duke and duchess had rented on the Rue de Blanchiserie, a former coachmaker's workshop, livery, and living quarters, was more than large enough to accommodate the 238 guests (103 0f whom were uniformed officers) as well as the many musicians, servants, and other staff required to stage such an event.

As the guests arrived, they were escorted to the Coach House, which had been converted into a giant ballroom for the night. Eager as ever to be at the heart of events, and to the musical accompaniment of a full orchestra, they were formally introduced to the 47-year-old duchess, even though she was already known to many of them. It was a grand occasion, if not to everyone's taste. The Reverend George Griffin Stonestreet wrote, somewhat disapprovingly:

> The severest etiquette is always present. The women upon entering salute one another upon each cheek with a kiss, they then sit down and remain as stiff as waxworks (seemingly

> indifferent to those around) while awaiting the invitation to dance. They always begin a ball with a perfect froideur (where distance is maintained) before they go on with a dangerous waltz. The English women like to finish with a gallop.

The women had their dance cards and the men their desires, as in the previously austere surroundings of the coach house chandeliers sparkled in the early evening gloom, brightly coloured garlands adorned recently papered walls, ribbons hung from the ceiling and rose petals littered the floor. In its heavily perfumed environs, with bows and curtsies aplenty, ladies in silk, taffeta and lace mingled with robust young men in a variety of military uniforms anxiously awaiting the invitation to dance.

However, regardless of the music, the gaiety, the flirtation, and the champagne-fuelled frivolity, there remained a tension in the air. The rumour persisted that Bonaparte was on the move. The army was prepared to march at moment's notice, but those present were reluctant to speak of it.

As the evening wore on it became increasingly humid and so the doors were thrown open to allow the gentle summer breeze to cool those perspiring

The Duchess of Richmond's Ball, Robert Alexander Hillingford (1870). (Goodwood House, Goodwood Art and Architecture)

from a vigorous waltz or military two-step. The Duchess of Richmond's daughter, Lady Louisa Lennox, recalled the scene:

> I well remember the Gordon Highlanders dancing reels at the Ball. My mother thought it would interest the foreigners to see them, which it did. I remember hearing that some of the poor men who danced in our house died in battle. There was quite a crowd to see the Scotch dancers.

The Duke of Wellington did not arrive until a little after 11pm, fashionably late perhaps, but there was a reason for his tardiness. Accompanied by his aides, he was the epitome of calm if somewhat brusque and unapproachable. Not long after, around the time supper was due to be served, a young officer, Harry Webster, arrived breathless and frantic. He had, he said, a letter for the Prince of Orange. The prince himself took receipt of the letter, but not wanting to cause alarm declined to read it, instead slipping it into his pocket.

Having been alerted to Webster's arrival, Wellington approached the prince and retrieved the letter. Upon reading it, although he remained unmoved, his countenance had changed.

The letter informed him that Bonaparte's army had broken camp and was on the move. This came as little surprise, but Wellington had believed that Napoleon would march west to disrupt his supply lines and threaten his route to the coast and any possible evacuation. Instead, Bonaparte had turned east, intending to prevent Wellington's army from linking up with the Prussians, under the command of Field Marshal Blücher. He intended, it seemed, to divide and conquer.

Wellington, exuding confidence, for there were many French spies in Brussels, with some no doubt some present at the ball, made his excuses and departed to an antechamber, where, perusing a map, he remarked to one of his staff officers: '*Napoleon has humbugged me, by God.*'

Wellington's army would make for Quatre Bras, but that would not be the place of decisive battle. Instead, he pointed to a location on the map, a small village called Waterloo, and declared, '*here we will make our stand.*'

The orchestra, which had ceased playing for a time, struck up once more, but by now the dancing was perfunctory at best as orders were issued and men began to leave.

The duchess wondered whether to curtail proceedings, but the duke insisted they continue. His young officers should experience the finery and delights of female companionship before war once again became the brutal landscape of their lives. But any frivolity was by now an illusion: the peace had been shattered, and the duke, after a few words intended to reassure, departed.

The Lady Georgiana de Ros remembered well the prevailing atmosphere:

> It was a dreadful evening; we were taking leave of friends and acquaintances many never to be seen again. The Duke of Brunswick made a speech as to the Brunswickers to be sure to distinguish themselves after the honour done to them by having the Duke accompany them to their review! I remember being quite provoked with poor Lord Hay, a dashing merry youth, full of military ardour, whom I knew very well for his delight at the idea of going into action, and all the honours he was to gain, but the first news that we received on the 16th was that he and the Duke of Brunswick were killed.

As the orders were passed around and salutes both given and received, the departure of the military men became an exodus. Those diplomats present likewise left in great haste and, as the coaches appeared in the courtyard, the clattering of horse's hooves on the cobblestoned streets soon drowned out the music of the orchestra. The strains of a waltz had given way to the noise of an army on the move. The Duchess of Richmond's youngest daughter recalled how, '*I suddenly became aware of the great preponderance of women in the room.*'

The atmosphere in the Rue de Blanchiserie had changed beyond recognition as Katherine Arden, the daughter of Lord Alvanley, who had arrived late to the ball, explained:

> On our arrival we were told that the troops had orders to march at three in the morning and that every officer must join his regiment by that time. Those who had brothers and sons to be engaged openly gave way to their grief, as the last of many farewells took place at this dreadful ball.

It seemed that the Duchess of Richmond's Ball, that highlight of the social calendar, had ended before it had even begun. Darkness descended and snuffed out the light and for many of those present a last chance for gaiety had passed that would never be repeated.

# Part Ten

# Scandal

# Chapter 1

# A Royal Marriage from Hell

George Augustus Frederick, Prince of Wales, was heir to the throne of Great Britain but this was no guarantee of respect. Indeed, in a life mired in scandal he became the most mocked, lampooned, and unpopular monarch in our history. He was so different from his austere and hard-working father, King George III.

As a young man George had been noted for his intelligence and razor-sharp wit. His repartee, it was said, was something to behold, whether drunk or sober. Unfortunately, by the time he was in his early twenties he was more often the former. Even so, he retained his admirers, if only for his good taste and love of fine things.

George was also physically attractive, if more pretty than handsome, but a dissolute lifestyle would soon take its toll. He lived extravagantly and considered himself to be what we would now call a style icon. One of his closest companions was the famous dandy, Beau Brummel.

Upon reaching the age of manhood George received an annual income from his father of £50,000 and a further £60,000 grant from Parliament. These huge amounts of money, equivalent to millions today, were barely ever enough to enough to cover his outgoings, as he commissioned and purchased Carlton House, reconstructed Windsor Castle, commissioned the building of Brighton Pavilion, held lavish parties, and lived in magnificent splendour. To the people he would come to rule he was a lazy, self-indulgent nitwit who squandered the nation's money.

This was not how George saw himself, however. As far as he was concerned he was the height of fashion, the finest prince in Europe and one of the leading men of his age. Yet he was regularly jeered at and verbally abused as he rode in his carriage through the streets of London. If he was a man worthy of respect, then he failed to convey these qualities to his people. He was a figure of ridicule and loathing and he struggled to understand why.

In 1783 George met and became besotted with Maria Fitzherbert, a twice-married Roman Catholic six years his senior. They very quickly became lovers and on 15 December they were married in a private ceremony.

As the heir to the throne, George was barred from marrying a Catholic by the Act of Settlement of 1701. He was also obliged, by the Royal Marriages Act of 1772, to obtain his father's permission to wed. At the time he was not on speaking terms with his father.

By 1787 the prince's debts were such that he was forced to go cap-in-hand to Parliament to bail him out, which they did, but only reluctantly. When he again expressed financial difficulties, he found Parliament less forthcoming and was forced instead to approach his father. Despairing of his son's indolence the king refused to help and only acquiesced once he had agreed to make a royal marriage.

The prince had only been kept solvent by the financial machinations of that master political manipulator Charles James Fox, who had since told him that he could do no more. He had little choice but to agree. The woman chosen to be his bride was Caroline of Brunswick.

Caroline's mother was the Princess Augustus, the king's sister and therefore Prince George's aunt. Caroline, then, was his first cousin. Despite this they had never met. She had been chosen not only because she was Protestant, but also because Brunswick, though only a small German principality, was a useful ally in Britain's ongoing rivalry with France.

On 20 November 1794, Lord Malmesbury arrived in Brunswick to escort the future queen to England. He was not impressed by what he saw, and noted in his diary that: '*she lacks judgement, decorum, and tact; speaks her mind too readily, acts indiscreetly and often neglects to wash or change her dirty clothes*'. Her father had earlier informed him that her education had been sorely neglected.

Malmesbury's attitude to Caroline was always ambivalent. He admired her honesty, her courage, and her natural rather than acquired morality, but she was entirely unsuitable as a bride for the wayward prince and he knew it. George was not one to hear home truths; he thrived on flattery. This often coarse, tactless, and plain-speaking young woman was unlikely to flatter his ego.

Caroline arrived in England on 5 April 1795 and was placed with Frances Villiers, Countess of Jersey, who had been made Her Lady of the Bedchamber and was at the time one of George's many mistresses. Her appointment caused the Duke of Wellington to later suggest that she had personally brought pressure to bear to ensure that Caroline was selected to be George's prospective bride to be, as a woman of such: '*Indelicate manners, indifferent character and not very inviting performance, from a hope that disgust with a wife would secure constancy to a mistress.*'

Caroline of Brunswick (1795). (Unknown author, georgianawordpress.com)

Upon meeting Caroline for the first time a clearly disappointed prince recoiled somewhat and ordered a large brandy. Caroline was no less disappointed in her intended and was to complain bitterly to Lord Malmesbury that the prince was very fat and nothing like as handsome as his portrait.

Once the formal introductions were over and it became abundantly clear the pair had nothing in common, they studiously avoided each other for the rest of the evening. From such unpromising beginnings things were only to get worse.

Nonetheless, the wedding of George, Prince of Wales and Caroline of Brunswick would proceed as planned, and so, amid much fanfare, on 8 April 1795 they were married in the Chapel Royal of St James' Palace.

George, who had already decided that his new wife was not only unattractive, but also unhygienic, was noticeably the worse for wear before he took his wedding vows. Indeed, Caroline was to claim that he was so inebriated on their wedding night that he passed out in the fireplace, where she left him.

George later revealed to a friend that he only had sex with his wife three times: twice on the first night and once on the second. He explained, '*It*

Wedding of George, Prince of Wales, and Princess Caroline of Brunswick, britainmagazine.com. (Public domain Wikimedia Commons)

*required no small effort on my part to conquer my aversion to her person.'* Despite a shared loathing of one another a daughter, the Princess Charlotte Augusta, did result from this brief and otherwise unsatisfactory union. A week after her birth George made his will, bequeathing all his worldly goods to Maria Fitzherbert while making provision for his wife of just one shilling.

It was clear there was no future in the marriage, and they were soon living apart, only ever communicating by letter. In the meantime, George sought to restrict Caroline's access to their daughter while desperately seeking an annulment of the marriage.

Refused permission to see her own daughter in 1802, Caroline adopted a three-month-old boy named William Austin, though a rumour, started by those close to the prince, it was said, soon began to circulate that he was in fact her illegitimate son by an unknown lover.

Still Caroline refused to be cowed by George's attempts to bully and intimidate her, even when, in 1806, under pressure from the prince, a Commission was established to investigate her behaviour. This was unable to discover anything improper, other than her general deportment.

In 1810 George III fell ill once more with porphyria, an illness undiagnosed at the time that made him delusional and seemingly mad. He had suffered from the illness intermittently for some time, but in years past had always recovered his senses. On this occasion he did not. As a result, the aged monarch was effectively retired, and his son George became Prince Regent to rule in his name.

In the meantime, Caroline was becoming the focus of opposition to the Prince Regent's lavish lifestyle and, unlike her husband who was roundly booed whenever he appeared in public, she was cheered wherever she went. The people liked her lack of pomposity, open familiarity, and warmed to the vulgarian streak that so appalled the social elite. The fact she was deprived of time with her daughter while the prince openly flaunted his mistresses in public, only served to reinforce her reputation as the wronged woman.

George, who had always been dismayed at his own unpopularity, was simply confounded by the love the people seemingly had for this dreadful woman, and her continued presence in the country haunted his every waking moment. Few might have sympathised with the prince and a dilemma that was at least in part of his own making, but what had been a mere inconvenience was fast becoming a constitutional crisis.

Caroline refused to countenance divorce or any reduction in her status, but after torturous negotiations she did agree to leave Britain and remain abroad for an annual allowance of £35,000. On 8 August 1810 she departed for the Continent, where she took up residence in a villa on the banks of Lake Como in Italy, before embarking on a tour of the Mediterranean with the man rumoured to be her lover, Bartolemeo Pergami. The affair caused a scandal and if true would be grounds for a divorce. In her absence the villa was ransacked by the prince's agents, but other than some rumpled and dirty bedclothes they could find no evidence of a relationship.

In November 1817, the Princess Charlotte Augusta died. George had neglected to tell Caroline of their daughter's illness, let alone her death, and she only found out by chance. She was devastated by the news and never forgave George his callous disregard for her feelings.

This was a time when divorce by mutual consent was not permissible in law and adultery either had to be proved or one of the parties involved had to admit to it. George, through his representatives, had been cajoling Caroline to consent to do this but there was no chance of that now.

On 29 January 1820, the aged and incapable George III died. It was clear now that following the Prince Regent's Coronation as King George IV, Caroline would be queen. A desperate George pleaded with his Parliament to prevent this but there was little they could do other than offer her a further £50,000 to stay away. She refused, telling them of her determination to attend the Coronation and take up her rightful role as queen of England.

When Caroline returned to England on 5 June 1821, it was to demonstrations of support, some of which verged on the riotous, but whereas her popularity with the people was a concern for the government, her mere presence infuriated the new king, who immediately revived his campaign against her and once again demanded a divorce on the grounds of her infidelities. The evidence he had accrued, most of it circumstantial, was now brought to Westminster for further investigation. Parliament had already introduced the Pains and Penalties Bill, which if passed would strip Caroline of her title as queen and dissolve the marriage. But that it seemed was not enough, and so the next legitimate queen of England was now effectively put on trial and her relationship with Bartolemeo Pergami made public.

Witnesses came forward to say that the couple had been seen kissing, and that Caroline was often in a state of undress in Bartolomeo's presence, and that there was only one bed in the villa they shared. But this was guilt by implication only, and the people just saw it as rank hypocrisy. George's affairs were common knowledge, as were the sexual indiscretions of other prominent public figures.

The Pains and Penalties Bill passed comfortably through the House of Lords, but it had little or no chance of passing the House of Commons, where the opposition to George was long standing and remained stubborn. To save the monarchy the humiliation of defeat the Bill was withdrawn.

The public inquiry into Caroline's private life had been a fiasco from the outset, and George's refusal to be reconciled with his wife and the government's collusion in his attempts to avoid doing so was making a laughing stock of them both. It is little wonder Caroline could joke: '*I have been accused of committing adultery with the husband of Mrs Fitzherbert.*'

The affair was no joke for the monarchy, as hundreds of petitions had been organised in Caroline's support, which gathered over a million signatures. She also campaigned hard on her own behalf and would address the crowds that would flock around her on every public appearance, telling them: '*As Queen, you will find in me a sincere friend to your liberties, and a zealous advocate of your rights.*'

Her words were fine and well received, but not entirely sincere, for she had already agreed to return abroad for the £50,000 previously offered. But she would only do so if permitted to attend the coronation and upon formal acknowledgement that she was queen. This George refused outright.

King George IV's coronation took place on 19 July 1821, a year later than intended, due to his unsuccessful attempt to exclude his wife from the ceremony.

Insisting that no expense be spared, the event was, as one can imagine from a man not given to understatement, a lavish affair, and Westminster Abbey was transformed for the ceremony. But no amount of artistry could distract from the presence of the person who would overshadow everything. George had prayed Caroline would not turn up, but she did.

Cheered by the crowds gathered outside on her arrival, she acknowledged their support before, accompanied by the head of her household Lord Hood, she tried to gain access to the abbey, only to find that on the orders of the Lord Chamberlain the doors had been locked and bolted against her. She walked around the abbey trying every available entrance. At one she was denied entry at bayonet point. At another she was asked for her invitation, to which she responded angrily '*I don't need an invitation; I am the Queen.*' She raised her voice, shook her fist and screamed profanities, but it made no difference. Eventually, in a state of high dudgeon, Lord Hood led her away with the crowd chanting 'Shame! Shame!' ringing in her ears.

Later that same night she fell seriously ill. Over the next two weeks her condition continued to deteriorate until finally, on 7 August, she died aged 53. The cause of her death remains unknown, but so sudden and unexpected was it that rumours persist that she was poisoned.

Buried in Brunswick, the inscription on her tomb read (at her insistence) '*Here lies Caroline, the Injured Queen of England.*'

Following Caroline's death, George IV's own health also went into steep decline. His devotion to the table saw his weight balloon while his heavy drinking led to mental decay and premature decrepitude. He found breathing difficult and would not rise from his bed for days on end. Indeed, by the age of sixty he was so obese that he rarely appeared in public, instead living in seclusion at Windsor Castle.

During George's reign the prestige and the popularity of the monarchy collapsed to an all-time low. The scandal of his marriage to Caroline of Brunswick was to dog him for the rest of his life and few people had a good word to say for him. Even the ultra-conservative Duke of Wellington felt moved to describe him as: '*The worst man I ever fell in with in my entire life, the most selfish, the most false, the most ill-natured, and the most entirely without one redeeming quality.*'

King George IV died on 26 June 1830, aged 67. *The Times* reported:

> There never was an individual less regretted by his fellow creatures than this deceased King. What eye has wept for him? What heart has heaved one sob of un-mercenary sorrow? Selfishness is the true repellent of human sympathy. Selfishness feels no attachment and invites none.

His queen would no doubt have concurred.

By the time the bloated and bedridden George IV, sustained in his delirium by a diet of brandy and laudanum, finally passed away, the monarchy had been reduced to a laughing stock, a joke to the man on the street, grist to the mill of the satirist's pen. The Georgian era, which had begun in trepidation but also hope, had ended in ridicule and farce.

Much like his brothers, who had sired dozens of children out of wedlock, George had bequeathed the nation no legitimate heir and so the crown passed to his younger sibling William, Duke of Clarence, who despite being personally responsible for ten of the aforementioned bastards, by dint of a distinguished military career did at least bring a thin veneer of respectability to the much-maligned institution.

# The End

Already 64 years of age, lame, but amiable, the new king could be said to have stopped the rot, but no more. Few could have imagined at the time that during the reign of his successor, a petite, plain, temperamental but strong-willed young woman, Britain would emerge as the first industrialised nation with mastery of the seas and the greatest empire the world had ever seen. Yet the Victorian era, named after the queen who presided over it, could not have been more different from the Georgian era that had given it birth. Indeed, it was a backlash against it. More abstemious times beckoned, in which propriety dominated and the making of money rather than the spending of it became the leitmotif of success and respectability. But the Victorians remain a story for another day and another book.